The Little
Mindfulness
Workbook

Everyday techniques to help you combat stress and
enhance your life

Gary Hennessey

breath
works

crimson

The Little Mindfulness Workbook: Everyday techniques to help you combat stress and enhance your life

This edition first published in Great Britain in 2016 by Crimson Publishing Ltd

19–21 Charles Street
Bath
BA1 1HX

British Library Cataloguing in Publication Data

A catalogue record for this book is available from the British Library.

ISBN 978 1 78059 154 4

Typeset by IDSUK (DataConnection) Ltd
Printed and bound in Malta by Gutenberg Press Ltd

*Dedicated to all my colleagues at Breathworks,
who work so hard to alleviate suffering*

Contents

Foreword

In *The Little Mindfulness Workbook*, Gary Hennessey has managed a feat that only true experts can achieve. He has written a book that is beautiful in its simplicity. With mastery comes an ability to hone a topic down to simple principles without losing depth and wisdom. Although this book is short, it is pithy. Although it is small, it is weighty. Although it contains a lot of common sense, it also hints at profound truths that can change your life forever.

I have had the great privilege to work with Gary for the past 15 years at Breathworks, the mindfulness organisation we founded along with our colleague, Sona Fricker. The early days were intensely creative as we debated topics, thrashed out issues and worked towards creating the finely tuned mindfulness courses we deliver today.

Over that period, I found Gary to have one of the most creative minds I have had the good fortune to work with. He has an astonishing ability to read widely and reflect deeply. He is at his happiest alone in his armchair reading, pondering – as well as sitting quietly doing nothing, surely one of the most difficult mindfulness practices of all! We are lucky enough to reap the benefits of his fine mind at work in the pure and lucid invitation to mindfulness provided in this book. You will never feel you are being talked at by an aloof expert. He writes in a human and approachable style. He comes across as a genial, warm and benevolent guide, offering to walk beside you as you delve into the mystery of what it means to be human and explore the wonder of having a mind and heart that is capable of change and transformation.

Vidyamala Burch
Co-founder of Breathworks
Author of *Mindfulness for Health*, *Mindfulness for Women* and *Living Well with Pain and Illness*

About the author

Gary Hennessey has been practising mindfulness for over 40 years, and has been teaching for 35. In 2002 he trained with Vidyamala Burch in teaching mindfulness to those with long-term health conditions. He is currently Breathworks Director of Training, and spends much of his time training people to become mindfulness teachers. He is the author – under his Buddhist name Ratnaguna – of *The Art of Reflection*.

Introduction

Mindfulness is a practical way of changing your life for the better. The principle underlying it is simple but profound: awareness is transformative. Bringing more awareness to our experience enables us to see how we make ourselves suffer unnecessarily, and seeing that gives us the possibility to stop doing it. More positively, it gives us the potential to start acting in ways that bring about more happiness, freedom and kindness into our lives.

You already possess that awareness to some degree, and mindfulness is simply a systematic way in which you can develop it further. This book describes how to do that.

Mindfulness was developed and taught by the Buddha – a man who lived in India over 2,500 years ago – who taught it as part of a spiritual discipline leading to enlightenment. However, the mindfulness that's being taught in secular contexts, and which I describe in this book, is a bit different from that taught by the

Buddha, and has a different purpose. This kind of mindfulness was developed by Jon Kabat-Zinn in the 1960s, and is now being taught in all sorts of contexts and for all sorts of purposes: as a way of living well with chronic pain and other physical long-term health conditions, to reduce stress, to prevent depression relapse, to prevent relapse into alcohol and/or drug use for those in recovery, in childbirth and parenting, in prisons, schools and the work environment, for eating disorders, to enhance performance in sport, and for victims of trauma, to name just a few.

It would be a mistake, though, to think that mindfulness is only a technique for dealing with problems or to improve some specific activity. It's also a very effective way of enhancing and enriching an already fairly happy life, as I know from my own experience.

How to use this book

The Little Mindfulness Workbook is designed so that you work gradually through the various exercises (which in mindfulness training are called practices), enabling you to experience the benefits of mindfulness for yourself. Each chapter builds on what you'll have learned in previous chapters, so it's a good idea to start at the beginning and work through to the end. You may want to read the book through first so that you know where you're going, or you can simply start practising right away.

There are many practices in this book and it's best not to rush through them, but to spend some time with each one before moving on to the next. Even when you move on to another practice, don't leave the previous ones behind, but continue to do them, so that over time you build a repertoire of practices, rather like a musician who learns many pieces of music.

I've taught the ideas and practices in this book to many people over a number of years, and I've invariably found that those who take the time to practise benefit greatly from them. Most people find that some practices work well for them immediately, while others seem not to. I say *seem* not to because it's not easy to know straight away whether or not a practice is helping us. We can only really know after doing it for some time. So I'd encourage you to keep giving all the practices in this book a try, even those you don't initially like – you may well find that you enjoy doing them at a later date.

Having said that, you'll naturally be drawn to those practices that are most congenial to you, and it's fine to home in on these. When my students tell me that they like a certain practice, I always encourage them to do lots of it, because if they like doing something, they're more likely to continue to practise. Pleasure is a strong motivator! But life, as you know, is not always easy and pleasant, and there will be times when being mindful feels like hard work. It's worth persevering at those times – our greatest insights into our behaviour often come when life is not going so well.

Ideas and practices

There are two main components of this book: ideas and practices. The ideas are, in a sense, the theory that underpins the practices – the *reasons* for practising mindfulness. They're more than just theory though, they're descriptions of experience, and by reading these descriptions you can begin to approach the experience yourself. Reading the ideas and letting them into your life is a necessary part of the work in this workbook.

The practices will help you with this, so after explaining an idea I'll give you something practical to do to help you experience it. Sometimes this will be something that you need do only once, which I'll call an *Enquiry*, but mostly they will be things that I recommend that you practise many times.

There are broadly two types of practice. The first is something that requires you to step out of your daily routine and spend some time focusing solely on practising without having to think about or do anything else. These practices are called *Meditations*. I'll be asking you to commit some time every day to this. How much time you commit is up to you. If you're new to meditation, then I'd suggest beginning with ten minutes, perhaps twice a day, and extending that as you get used to practising and feel like doing more.

If our practice was restricted to meditation alone, though, we'd be mindful for quite a short period every day. What we're aiming for is to be mindful more or less all the time, and at the end of most chapters I'll give you simple things you can do while going about your daily business. I've called these practices *Mindfulness in action*. If you practise these, and keep practising them, by the time you get to the end of the book you'll be mindful for quite a lot of the time.

The way practice works

One of the great practical discoveries of neuroscience is that the brain changes with experience. Say you were learning to dance, for instance: when you learn a new dance step, a new neural pathway is created that gives instructions to your body on how to perform that step. Of course, doing it just once isn't going to make you a good dancer, but practising that step over and over strengthens that neural pathway, changing your brain, making the step easier to perform, and making you better at it. This happens not just for physical actions; our brain changes whenever we think, imagine, or feel something repeatedly. So, as you do the practices I describe in this book you're actually changing your brain – developing and strengthening new neural pathways – which of course means changing your mind and your experience. Studies have shown that mindfulness reduces stress, decreases anxiety, increases emotional resilience, strengthens the immune system and lifts mood, to mention just a few benefits.

An eight-week mindfulness course

You could, if you wished, use this book as an eight-week course. My colleagues and I have run a very successful course for many years using the material in this book, and we have evidence of its efficacy. If you'd like to do it in eight weeks, each chapter from Chapter 2 onwards represents a week of the course. At the end of each chapter your practice for the week is listed. At the end of the book, on page 167, I've also summarised the practices you would do each week, so that you can see at a glance what you should be doing. Of course, you don't need to do it in eight weeks, you can take as long as you want to, but it's an option for you.

Recordings of the meditations in this book

You can listen to me and some of my collegaues guiding the meditations described in this book wherever you see this symbol 🔊 by going to https://soundcloud.com/breathworks-mindfulness/sets/the-little-mindfulness-workbook. If you have a smartphone, put the meditations on it so that you can listen to them anywhere.

Keeping a journal

It can be helpful to write a journal to keep a track of how you're getting on with your practice of mindfulness. You could buy a notebook especially for this purpose, or you could download journal templates from www.breathworks-mindfulness.org.uk/the-little-mindfulness-workbook, which include the specific practices introduced in each chapter of this book. ✎

1

What is mindfulness?

Rather than tell you straight out what mindfulness is, I'm going to guide you in a mindfulness exercise or enquiry so that you can experience it for yourself, after which we'll review that experience and draw out some principles.

To do this you'll need to get yourself a cup of tea or whatever you like to drink. I'll refer to it as a cup of tea throughout, so if you're drinking something else, just adapt what I write to your particular drink.

Note: In all the following enquiries and meditations I describe, I often give an instruction followed by an ellipsis: '...' . This signifies that you close your eyes and spend a little time exploring the instruction I've just given. For instance, when I write 'Then become aware of the breath …', don't go straight to the next instruction, but spend some time being aware of your breath. After a little while – how much time is up to you – open your eyes and read the next instruction. If you're listening to an audio recording of the enquiry or meditation, then of course you can keep your eyes closed the whole time.

Enquiry 1: drinking a cup of tea

First, just hold the cup or mug in your hand and gaze at it … Notice the way the light and shade falls on it … Is it lighter on one side than on the other? … Notice how it reflects light, and the different colours the reflections give to it. For instance, if it's a white mug, is it just one shade of white all over, or is it many shades, many colours? …

Now look at the surface of the tea itself. Notice the colours, the reflections, the shades … Notice the steam coming off it …

Now *feel* it in your hand, the sensations on your skin, the heat, the weight of it ...

Now bring it up to your nose and breathe in – does it have an aroma? Perhaps close your eyes to better concentrate on its smell ... it may be strong, or it may be very subtle ...

As you're doing this you'll probably also feel the steam on your face ... If you want to feel that more fully, put the cup underneath your chin ...

If you're thirsty, notice the feeling of wanting to drink ... Be curious about that sensation ... What does thirst feel like? What does the urge to do something feel like? ...

Maybe there's some impatience too, what does that feel like? ...

OK, bring the cup to your mouth ... feel the rim of the cup on your lips ... what does that feel like? Now take a sip, and hold the liquid in your mouth for a few seconds ... what does liquid feel like? And the taste? ...

Now swallow if you haven't already done so. Feel the drink slip down your throat ... The feeling of satisfaction as you do so ...

If you were more or less following my instructions just then you were practising mindfulness. So let's review what you did. First, **you paid attention**. You paid attention to how the cup looked, how it felt in your hand, its temperature. You also paid attention to the tea itself, what it looked like, its aroma, and its taste.

So, **you used more than one sense**. You looked, felt, smelled and tasted. If it had had a sound I would have asked you to listen to it, too (a cup of tea doesn't have a sound unless you happen to drop it!). Mindfulness is being aware with all of our senses. The word mindfulness can easily be misunderstood because we tend to associate the mind with thinking, so we may assume that mindfulness means thinking. We *can* be mindful of our thoughts, but mindfulness doesn't necessarily mean thinking. **Mindfulness is being aware of our experience**, whatever that may be.

Experience always occurs in the present moment. We can remember experiences of course, and we can anticipate them, but the actual experience only happens in the present. Not that being mindful prevents you from using your memory or planning for the future. Of course it can be useful to do both those things, but our minds tend to slip off to the past or the future without us really being aware that it's happened, which means that we miss a lot of our life in an abstracted state, not really being here, not fully experiencing our own life as it happens. It would probably be shocking if we were able to add up all the times when we'd been distracted from what was actually happening around or within us. How much of our life have we missed? I recently read that the average adult spends three and a half years of their life driving a car. I wonder how many years the average adult spends not really being here?

Did your mind wander off at any point in the exercise? If it did, there was probably a point at which you noticed it, when you kind of 'came to' – 'Ah yes, I'm supposed to be doing this exercise' – and I expect you then came back to awareness of the cup of tea.

Anyone who practises mindfulness does this a lot. There may be a few rare people who manage to remain mindful all of the time, but for most of us **mindfulness consists largely in 'coming back' to the present moment**.

Definitions of mindfulness

So now, based on that experience, we can approach a definition of mindfulness. Here's one I like, from a meditation teacher called Dharmachari Bodhipaksha:

Mindfulness is the gentle effort to be continuously present with experience.

It does take some effort to be mindful, it takes a little effort to come back to our experience again and again, but the effort is gentle. Rather like the effort needed to bring a small child back to the dinner table. Of course we can get impatient with the child and bring her back harshly, perhaps shout at her, but that isn't the best or kindest way to do it. Similarly, we can get frustrated with our minds and pull them back impatiently and forcibly, but in mindfulness practice we bring ourselves back gently, with patience. Notice that it's not the effort to *control* our experience, or *have any particular kind* of experience, it's simply the effort to *pay attention* to our experience, whatever it is.

This definition doesn't capture everything, though. If you already know something about mindfulness you'll probably have come across this well-known definition from Jon Kabat-Zinn:

Mindfulness is paying attention in a particular way; on purpose, in the present moment, and non-judgementally.

'Non-judgementally' refers to the automatic tendency most of us have to constantly judge experiences, situations, other people – ourselves! – as being good or bad, valuable or worthless. Not that we should never make judgements – of course we have to – but paying attention non-judgementally means we let go of the automatic tendency to judge things in a very black-and-white way: 'This is good, this is bad; I like this, I don't like that.' Letting go of this judging mindset allows us to get closer to seeing things as they are – neither black nor white, usually, but varying shades of colour. In mindfulness practice we use the word *discerning* for the sensitive noticing of differences in experience – as you did when being mindful of the cup of tea – and we reserve the word *judging* for the tendency to divide experience into two separate categories and then accept one and reject the other. As you begin to practise mindfulness you'll probably notice the tendency to be judgemental and then you'll have to be careful not to be judgemental about that! Instead, simply notice what the mind does with curiosity and humour: 'How interesting, there I go being judgemental again.' As you notice this tendency you'll find that, in time, it gently drops away.

Autopilot

Probably most of the time you don't pay as much attention to drinking a cup of tea as you did just now. Usually, we drink while working, talking, thinking about something else, watching the TV, reading the newspaper, so we don't actually *notice* drinking. I expect you've had the experience of having drunk a cup of tea and not remembering drinking it – 'Where did that tea go?' – or coming across a cold cup of tea that you made two hours ago! I wonder how many great taste experiences you've missed because you weren't paying attention? This is probably true for many of the routine things we do; things that don't require our full attention – eating, walking, driving, washing up – we tend to do on autopilot.

At first sight perhaps autopilot seems like a good thing. If we can do simple tasks automatically, freeing up our mind to do other things, doesn't that mean we can be more efficient?

Yes, it does in some ways, but it also has its drawbacks. When we're running on autopilot we react to things that happen to us in habitual ways – it's like having our buttons pressed. If we're prone to anxiety, say, the chances are that when we're on autopilot our mind will have anxious thoughts and we won't notice. We'll be 'lost' in those thoughts. This means that once we come back to awareness, we find that we're feeling really anxious and we don't know why – we don't know how we got there.

Now that you've had a little experience of mindfulness, and you have some understanding of it, let's try another enquiry. In this one we'll try to be mindful of the physical sensations in a particular part of the body.

Enquiry 2: being aware of the sensations in a part of your body

Choose a part of your body to focus your attention on – it could be the soles of your feet, your hands, your face, or wherever. If you feel like it, you can close your eyes to do this; it may help you to focus your mind and not get distracted by things you can see around you.

Pay attention to whichever part of your body you've chosen ... Feel whatever sensations may be present there ... We're not *thinking about* that part of the body, or visualising it, but noticing and feeling whatever sensations are there ...

Perhaps there aren't any sensations? ... OK, just notice that, but be open to the possibility that sensations may arise as you pay attention to it ...

If your mind wanders, simply bring it back when you've noticed, but gently, patiently ...

Do this for five minutes or so.

So what happened there? Were you able to feel any sensations? If you couldn't feel anything, how did you feel about that? Did your mind wander? Or maybe you got bored? A common experience among people new to mindfulness is a sense that they aren't doing it correctly. If their mind wanders, or they don't feel any sensations in the body, or they don't feel calm, they think they must be doing it wrong. This is an aspect of the judging mind that I mentioned earlier: right and wrong, success and failure. But one of the liberating aspects of mindfulness is that you can't really do it wrongly. If you're being mindful, then you're doing it right. This is because we aren't trying to have any particular experience, we're just noticing what our experience happens to be. So, if your mind wanders and you notice that, if you're not calm but agitated and you notice that, if you don't feel any sensations in the body and you notice that, then you're being mindful.

OK, so now, if you've got time, why not have another go? Be mindful of another part of your body and this time, know that you're doing it perfectly!

Your experience

Write down what you noticed as you were doing this enquiry. What physical sensations were present? Did any thoughts come into your mind, did you notice any feelings, and did you have any judgements about the practice, or yourself doing the practice?

Physical sensations: ....

....

Thoughts: ....

....

Feelings: ....

....

Judgements: ....

....

2 Learning to choose

Idea: Reacting and responding

One of the reasons it's worth practising mindfulness is because it gives us more choice. Not necessarily any more choice in what happens *to* us, but in how we respond to what happens. For instance, you might feel irritated whenever you're caught in a traffic jam or your train is running late. Of course getting irritated by such things doesn't help: it's an unpleasant state to be in and no matter how irritated and impatient we become, it will not clear the traffic or speed up the train. Our irritation can also turn to anger, which then might spill out into our communication, which in turn might have a bad effect on our relationships with others.

When we habitually react to certain situations it feels as if that's the only possible reaction to have. For someone who always gets irritated when stuck in traffic or waiting for a late train, irritation may seem to be the natural and reasonable thing to feel. Traffic jams and late trains = irritation! This isn't true of course, as the irritated person could see if he or she were to look around at the other drivers or passengers around them, some of whom may be chatting unconcernedly, singing along to a tune on their radio, or laughing at a joke. There *are* other possible ways to respond, which means that we don't *have* to react in the way that we habitually do.

When we become aware that our irritation is not actually caused by the traffic or the late train, but is our own personal reaction to it, then choice becomes possible – shall I allow myself to be irritated as usual or shall I respond in a different way? You may have noticed that I'm using the words react and respond in very specific ways here: a reaction is usually not conscious but automatic and habitual, while a response is conscious, chosen and creative.

The first step in moving from reaction to response is to notice what's actually happening. Being caught in traffic or waiting for a late train is – for most of us, most of the time – an *unpleasant experience*. What do we do – what does our mind do – when our experience is unpleasant? We look for a way out. When stuck in a traffic jam, for instance, you might try to find an alternative route. Let's say you do that and you find that route is blocked too. Now what does your mind do?

If you're anything like me or anyone else I know, you'll find it hard to accept the situation and do as the song recommends: 'Don't worry, be happy!' Especially if you're on your way to an important meeting or dying to get home. We instinctively *resist* unpleasant experiences, even when there's nothing we can do to change them, and this resistance is expressed in thoughts, emotions and judgements. If you're stuck in a traffic jam, for instance, you might be thinking 'Why is there a traffic jam here at this time of the day?', 'This is ridiculous', 'Come on, get a move on'; you might be feeling irritated, angry, guilty (at not leaving earlier), anxious (about missing an appointment), upset (about the possibility that your children will be asleep by the time you get home); and you may be having certain judgements about the situation: 'There are too many cars on the roads these days', 'Why do they have to dig up the road *again*!', 'The transport minister is hopeless'.

These kinds of reactions tend to escalate, one thought leading to others, leading to more emotions, leading to more judgements, leading to more thoughts, etc. So our resistance to unpleasant experience merely adds another layer of suffering to it. A layer of suffering that we don't need to have.

We can call our direct experience primary and all the reactions to that we can call secondary experience. Mindfulness practice consists in distinguishing between our primary and secondary experience, and then letting go of the secondary and simply being

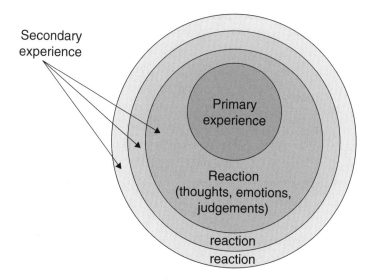

Secondary experience

Primary experience

Reaction
(thoughts, emotions, judgements)

reaction

reaction

with the primary experience. In the case of being stuck in a traffic jam, our primary experience is simply one of sitting in a stationary car, wanting it to be able to move. That's all that's happening. This is obviously unpleasant, and mindfulness won't make that OK or turn it into a pleasant experience, but at least you won't have to endure the escalation of thoughts, emotions and judgements on top of that. Secondary suffering is optional!

The difference between feelings and emotions

Usually we use the words feelings and emotions interchangeably, but for the purposes of this book I'm going to distinguish between them in the following way. Feelings are simply what experiences *feel* like, while emotions are what we *do* with those feelings. Emotions are reactions or responses to experiences and events. Say you've just discovered that your train is going to be an hour late. You'll probably *feel* disappointed, dismayed, frustrated, maybe even distressed if it means you're going to miss something that's important to you. But let's say you get angry about it – that's an *emotion*. We have no choice in how we feel, but we *can* learn to choose our emotional responses. Getting angry is reactive, whereas accepting the situation with grace and humour is a response.

Learning to distinguish primary and secondary experience

At first it can be hard to disentangle primary from secondary experience, especially when we're in a situation in which we tend to react, so let's have a go now. Remember, primary experience is your *direct* experience, what it *feels, looks, sounds, smells or tastes* like. Secondary experience is made up of your thoughts, emotions and judgements *about* your primary experience. First, write down the aspects of your current primary experience in the left-hand column. Then write down the aspects of your secondary experience in the right-hand column.

Primary experience	Secondary experience

Meditation: The body scan

Meditation – at least the kind you'll learn in this book – is of the same nature as the mindful enquiries I introduced in Chapter 1. That is, when we meditate we simply pay close attention to our experience, just as it is. We get up close to it, we become intimate with it. We don't try to change it, we don't strive to reach any particular goal, we don't try to have any specific experience. We just pay attention to our experience as it is in the present moment, non-judgementally. As I wrote in the Introduction, awareness is transformative. When we pay close attention to our experience it tends to change: if we're agitated, for instance, when we pay attention to that agitation, and if we don't judge it, it tends to calm down naturally. I'll say more about this process in Chapter 5.

Meditation helps us to be with – and stay with – our primary experience, and it helps us to let go of secondary experience. Much of our primary experience is felt in the body, so we begin by meditating on the sensations in the body.

The body scan

This is an extended version of the enquiry you did earlier when you were being aware of the sensations in a particular part of your body. You'll need about 20 minutes to do this, so try to make sure you won't be disturbed. It's usually done lying down, although it can be done sitting. When lying down, lie on something that's comfortable but firm, so that it supports you. This can be your bed if it is quite firm, or a thick mat on the floor. Put a cushion or pillow underneath your head, so that your neck is not tight or cramped. If you have a lower back problem you may find it more comfortable to have a couple of cushions beneath your knees, or have your legs bent, with the soles of the feet on the ground; otherwise, you can have your legs outstretched. Your arms can either be lying down at your sides, with the palms facing upwards, or you can rest your hands lightly on the stomach, with the palms facing downwards.

If you'd rather sit, go to pages 40–46 for tips on posture.

Your body temperature will probably drop as you lie or sit still during the practice, so try to make sure you'll be warm enough. Perhaps cover yourself with a light blanket, or have one beside you in case you need it.

Meditation 1: the body scan

First, become aware of your body as a whole, from the head to the toes ... Feel its weight against the mats or the floor beneath you ... Have a sense of the whole of your body: its weight, its temperature, how it feels ...

Then become aware of the breath ... feel it entering and leaving the body ... Feel the chest and the stomach rising and falling as the breath comes in and goes out ... You may notice other parts of the body moving slightly with the breath – the back, the shoulders, even the arms or legs ...

Now take your attention to each part of the body, letting your awareness rest in each part for a while. You can start with the head and work slowly down the body to the feet, or vice versa. As you become aware of each area, see if you can accept whatever sensations are present. Some parts may feel relaxed, warm and comfortable, while others may feel tense, uncomfortable or even painful. Some other parts may feel numb. The practice is just to feel whatever sensations are there, just as they are ...

If the sensations are pleasant, see if you can experience them without trying to hold onto them. If they are unpleasant, as best you can, accept them without trying to push them away, breathing into them, softening around them ...

Once you've moved through the whole body in this way, broaden your awareness to include your whole body once again ...

Sit or lie for a few moments, doing nothing at all, and then mindfully get up and see if you can take this awareness into the rest of your day.

So, how was that? Numerous opportunities to notice the mind wandering off and to bring it gently back! If you have discomfort or pain anywhere then doing the body scan probably made you even more aware of it, and you may have wondered about the value of that. Why pay attention to pain and discomfort? I'm going to ask you to hold that question for now. There *is* great value in it, and if you're willing to persevere, you'll begin to feel and understand it for yourself.

Your experience

Write down what you noticed about your experience of the body scan.

Physical sensations: ....

....

Thoughts: ....

....

Feelings: ....

....

Mindfulness in action 1: do one routine activity mindfully every day

Choose an activity – something that you normally do at least once every day, such as cleaning your teeth, having a shower, eating a meal, opening and/or closing doors, walking up and/or down stairs, drinking a cup of tea or coffee.

Whatever activity you choose, don't do it on autopilot, but pay full attention to it.

Let's take as an example cleaning your teeth. Paying attention means, first of all, *just* cleaning your teeth, and not doing something else as well, such as cleaning the sink at the same time, or wandering out of the bathroom to continue a conversation (rather awkwardly) with a family member. It means not multi-tasking.

It also means paying attention to what it *feels* like: the feeling of the brush on your teeth and gums, of the toothpaste in your mouth, of the fresh water as you rinse your mouth at the end, and the taste of the toothpaste of course. Taste it!

It means bringing your mind back to what you're doing whenever it wanders on to something else, which it probably will do a number of times, even in a two-minute session of cleaning your teeth.

I've used the example of cleaning your teeth, but you can bring the same ideas to bear on whatever activity you choose to be mindful in: eating a meal, drinking a cup of tea, going up and down stairs, whatever.

- Do just the activity, and nothing else
- Pay attention to the physical sensations of doing it
- Bring your mind back whenever it wanders

Practise doing this every day for a week.

How did that go? Actually you're probably reading this before you've practised it! Never mind – read this again in a week's time ...

So, assuming that you've done this for a week now, how was it? Did you remember to do it? The biggest barrier to doing this practice is forgetting to do it. Don't worry if you did forget – we're practising non-judgemental awareness, aren't we? So you can have another go this week. Or perhaps you remembered to do it a few times, or even just once. If so, what was it like? Were you able to remain mindful throughout the whole of the activity? What, if anything, did you notice?

Now choose another activity and do it mindfully for the next few days. Ideally *in addition* to the one you've just done. The idea here is that you gradually build up a number of mindful activities, and eventually you'll 'join the dots' and be mindful all the time.

Summary

In this chapter, I've introduced the distinction between primary and secondary experience, and we've seen that when our primary experience is unpleasant or challenging, we tend to react in unhelpful ways. Mindfulness enables us to become aware of our reactions, which allows us to have some choice in whether to react or to respond.

Practice

I've introduced two practices, the body scan and doing an activity mindfully. Practise these every day, or at least as many days as you can manage, for the next week.

 To download a template of a journal for this chapter's practice go to www.breathworks-mindfulness.org.uk/the-little-mindfulness-workbook.

3 Coming to your senses

Idea: Doing and being

A useful distinction that we make in mindfulness practice is between *doing* and *being* modes of mind. Doing mode is the mindset that strives after goals. It's not satisfied with the way things are right now, but tries to improve them. It notices problems and tries to fix them. Therefore, doing mode tends to be future-oriented, working towards the goals it has set, the improvements it wants to make, the problems it tries to solve.

Being mode is oriented to the present moment. When we're in being mode we experience the present moment directly in all its fullness and richness – and imperfection – and we don't feel any great need to change it or achieve anything. Instead, we're interested in and curious about our experience.

Generally speaking, most people spend a lot more time in doing than they do in being mode, and in mindfulness practice we try to shift the balance towards being. You might think this sounds very passive, that mindfulness involves letting things just be as they are, even if those things are substandard, unjust or cause suffering. However, being mode does lead to change – often to profound and far-reaching change – but it does so in a different way from doing mode. You'll discover for yourself how being mode enables change as you work through this book, but if you want an explanation now, go to page 95 and read the section on *The paradox of mindfulness*.

Human being or human doing?

Recollect the last few days and record in the left-hand column all the times when you were in doing mode. These might include cleaning your home, working, travelling to and from work, shopping. Then record in the right-hand column all the times when you were in being mode. These might include watching a film, listening to music, talking to a friend, doing nothing in particular.

Doing mode	Being mode

OK, and which mode are you in right now?

Meditation: Mindfulness of breathing

Meditation is a practice in being mode. We simply pay close attention to whatever our experience happens to be, not trying to get into any particular state or change whatever is happening. In the 'mindfulness of breathing' meditation on page 46, we pay attention to the sensations of the breath in the body. We don't try to breathe in any particular way, we just feel and observe the breath as it is in its natural state.

Whereas the 'body scan' meditation (page 29) is usually done lying down, this meditation is better done sitting upright. As you'll be sitting still for ten minutes or so, it's important to find a posture that you can comfortably hold for that long.

Meditation posture

The main criteria in finding a posture for meditation are that the body should be subjected to as little muscular strain as possible and that it supports an alert but relaxed state of mind. Let's look at three different ways to sit.

Sitting on a chair

It's best to choose a chair that is straight-backed, such as a dining chair. If you sit in an armchair or on a couch, your body will tend to slump and then you're likely to feel sleepy. Your shoulders will tend to round inwards, constricting the chest area, and this can bring about an emotional dullness. An upright chair helps the spine to follow its natural curves, creating a sense of openness in the chest that encourages alertness and emotional brightness.

Another way to maintain uprightness and avoid slumping is to rest your hands lightly in your lap, perhaps resting a cushion beneath them to raise their height a little. That allows the shoulders to remain open and broad, and they won't be drawn downwards or forwards by the weight of the hands as the meditation progresses. See image on the following page.

Make sure your feet are flat on the floor. If your feet don't reach the ground then place a cushion or pillow under them.

Kneeling on the floor

For this posture you'll need a couple of firm cushions to sit on, cushions that won't squash to almost nothing when you sit on them. If you don't have any firm cushions, you could take some books and place a cushion or two on top of them, with your legs astride the cushions.

Kneeling on the floor is a bit harder on the knees and ankles, so you'll just have to see what feels best for you. If you do kneel, it's important to find the right height. If the cushions are too high, your pelvis will tend to tip forwards, over-arching the lower back; if it's too low, your pelvis will tend to roll backwards, rounding the back and shoulders. Both extremes produce an unhelpful posture and may produce back pain, neck pain and an overall sense of strain. So paying attention to the height of your seat is important.

If you get strain in your ankles when you kneel you can try supporting them with rolled up socks or something similar that takes the strain off the ankle joint. Play around with what you have to hand and see if you can get comfortable.

Sitting cross-legged

The final option is to sit cross-legged on the floor. To do this comfortably your hips need to be quite flexible. Sit on a firm cushion and let your knees touch the floor, allowing your weight to be held by both the knees as well as the bottom. Can you do that comfortably? If not, then sitting cross-legged is probably not for you. Don't sit with your knees in the air, and definitely don't sit with your knees higher than your hips. It's very difficult to keep a straight back in these cases, and you'll end up slumped over uncomfortably.

As with the chair and kneeling postures, try to sit with a straight back, and to do this you'll need to experiment with different sizes of cushions. Support your hands either in your lap, perhaps on a small cushion, or on the tops of your thighs. Try to make sure your chest is open, and that your head is balanced nicely on your neck – neither looking down nor up – so that your neck muscles have little work to do.

Sometimes you may need to alter your posture within a meditation session, but if you do move, include that in your meditation, moving mindfully.

OK, so I think we're ready to meditate now.

Meditation 2: the mindfulness of breathing

Sit in a comfortable, upright posture. Spend a little time becoming aware of your body, the sensations of contact with the chair or cushion and the floor ... feel that contact ...

Can you feel your clothes resting on your skin? ...
Can you feel the air temperature on your skin? ...

Notice all sensations, and allow them to be just as they are, whether pleasant or unpleasant, or somewhere in between ...

Now rest your awareness on the sensations of breathing ... your chest expanding and contracting ... your belly swelling and subsiding ... your abdomen ...

Whenever your mind wanders, once you notice that, bring it back to your breath, gently and patiently ...

Now take your attention to your back ... the back also moves as we breathe, although these movements are quite subtle ... if you're sitting with your back supported, perhaps by the back of a chair, you may notice how the feeling of contact with that support changes as you breathe in and out ... stay with the movements in your back for a while ...

How about your shoulders ... can you feel any movement there? ...

Now broaden your awareness, so that you're aware of the whole of your torso moving gently with the breath ...

Now take your awareness to the place where you feel the air first entering your body ... if you're breathing through your nose, that will be the tip of your nose, or your upper lip or inside the nostrils ... if you're breathing through your mouth, that will be the lips, the tongue or the roof of the mouth ...

These sensations are quite subtle and you may not feel them at first. However, if you continue to pay attention to them, you'll begin to feel them ... Allow your attention to be light and subtle, like a butterfly resting on a flower ...

Now broaden your awareness once again to include the whole of your body ... Sit for a few moments, letting go of all effort ...

Now open your eyes, and begin to move. See if you can retain some of the awareness of your breath as you go about your day.

Your experience

Write down what you noticed when you did the mindfulness of breathing.

Physical sensations: ....

....

Thoughts: ....

....

Feelings: ....

....

Idea: Sensing more, thinking less

One of the things you'll have noticed is that mindfulness practice consists largely in being aware of - *experiencing* - the body. This is because we're interested in having a direct experience of life, rather than one mediated by thoughts and ideas. In the diagram opposite (adapted from work by Professor Mark Williams)[1] the left-hand triangle represents our direct experience of the world - the world we see, hear, touch, etc; the right-hand triangle represents our conceptualisation of that world - the way we label every experience, and then think about, analyse, compare, judge it, etc.

Most of us tend to spend quite a lot of time in the upper half of the diagram, with some awareness of our direct experience, but quite a lot of thinking *about* it. When we experience problems in life, or are unhappy or stressed, we tend to operate at the higher end of the diagram - in the band marked X - worrying, analysing, problem-solving, etc. The ability to think, analyse and reflect is a wonderful thing, but when we're stressed or unhappy we tend to

---

1   From M. Williams, 'Mindfulness and Psychological Process', *Emotion*, 2010, Vol. 10, No. 1, 1–7.

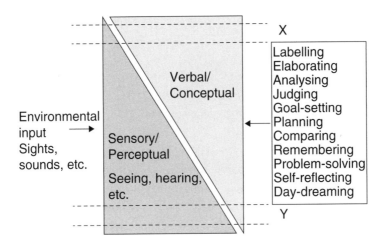

overuse this part of our mind, and this mental activity keeps us trapped in the very problems we're trying to solve.

Mindfulness helps us to move towards the lower end of the diagram, with a more direct experience of the world, and less (fruitless) thinking. The band marked Y at the lower end of the diagram represents a high degree of sensory experience with very little thought. To have this experience we don't have to make an effort to think less; if we pay attention to our direct sensory experience there's simply no room left in our mind for thinking *about* it.

It's not that we're aiming to live all the time in band Y – sometimes it's appropriate to think, after all – we're just trying to live from a more direct, immediate experience of the world.

There's a connection here with doing and being. Doing mode tends to keep us in the upper part of the diagram, with much analysing, evaluating, comparing, goal-setting, problem-fixing. Being mode tends to operate in the lower part, in which we're aware of all of our experience through the five senses, deeply embedded in our actual felt experience. Thought *is* included in being mode, but not over-conceptualisation, and our thinking is connected with our experience. We could call it embodied thought.

Slow down a bit

One way to move down the two triangles – to switch from doing to being mode – is to do things a little more slowly than we usually do. This helps to move us out of the attitude of doing things only in order to get them done, and allows us to appreciate the doing of them, to enjoy the journey as well as the destination, as the old saying goes.

Being mindful doesn't necessarily mean doing everything slowly – it's possible to be mindful *and* quick – but when we do things quickly there is a tendency to go into our heads, to go into *doing* mode.

Also, doing everything quickly has quite a bad effect on you in the long run. It activates the stress-response system, releasing adrenaline and cortisol into your bloodstream. These hormones weaken your immune system over time, and they also lower your mood. It activates the 'alarm system' in your brain, so that you're on the lookout for threats, making you prone to finding things to worry about and get irritated with, which means it's easier to react, harder to respond.

Mindfulness in action 2: do a few things more slowly than usual

For instance, when you have a cup of tea, take some time to drink it. Bring the cup slowly up to your lips, sip it slowly as if you had all the time in the world. Taste it. Enjoy it.

If you're walking somewhere, leave in plenty of time so that your walk doesn't become yet another thing you have to do quickly. Walk slowly, looking around you, noticing things.

If you drive a car, try driving more slowly than usual.

Do a job slowly – give yourself the time to do it meditatively, without rush, without haste.

Read a book slowly, giving yourself time to savour the prose, the ideas. You might even give yourself time to pause and reflect on what the author has written. Luxuriate in the slowness!

You may notice that it's difficult to do something more slowly than usual – once we've become used to doing something quickly it's hard to do it at a slower pace. Notice the urge to speed up, get it done and wrapped up, the sense of future orientation, the mind's urge to move on to the next thing, rather than being here in the moment.

Summary

In this chapter, I've introduced two related ideas: *doing* and *being*, and *perceptual* and *conceptual* modes of mind. It's common for people to spend most of their time in doing and conceptual modes, and an important aspect of mindfulness practice is to cultivate being and perceptual modes.

Practice

I've also introduced two new practices: the mindfulness of breathing meditation, and doing something more slowly than usual. Add these to the practices you learned in the previous chapter. So you could, for instance, alternate the body scan and mindfulness of breathing meditations, and you could do something slowly *as well as* doing a routine activity mindfully.

 To download the template of a journal for this chapter's practice go to www.breathworks-mindfulness.org.uk/the-little-mindfulness-workbook.

4 Working with thoughts

Idea: You don't have to believe everything you think

If you're new to meditation you may be surprised at the number of thoughts that come into your mind in the space of ten minutes. You may even suspect that meditating is making you think more than you did before you took up the practice. This is actually very unlikely. The average person has thousands of thoughts per day, so it's more likely that you've been thinking all the time, and that meditating has simply made you aware of it.

A common misconception of meditation is that it's about 'emptying the mind of thoughts' or 'making the mind a blank', and if you've been trying to achieve this then the chances are that you've been failing, in which case you're probably feeling a little frustrated and demoralised, and may be wondering if you'll ever really be able to meditate 'properly'.

Trying to stop our stream of thoughts is like King Canute ordering the tide to stop - it's doomed to failure. So what *are* we to do with them? Let's return to the diagram of the two triangles on page 51. There I said that we tend to live in the upper part of the diagram (lots of thoughts), and in mindfulness practice we gradually move down into a more direct experience of the world through the five senses. I said that to do this we don't have to try to stop thinking, because by paying attention to our direct, physical experience, our thoughts naturally quieten down.

However, you may have noticed that it's not as easy as that may sound. Our thoughts are compelling - they seem to want us to take notice of them.

In this cartoon, the person standing on the bridge is you, the bridge is meditation - or we could say your direct experience in the present moment – and the train passing underneath is your train of thoughts. It's a goods train, with open wagons, each of them carrying a different thought. We can't stop the train from passing, nor do we have to try, instead we simply notice the wagons as they come into view, and let them go. What we often

do, of course, is jump into one of the wagons; we get involved in a thought and let it take us away from the present moment.

Another way of putting this is that in mindfulness practice we look *at* our thoughts rather than *from* them. Usually, when we have a thought we tend to take it seriously, we believe what it's telling us, and we then look at the world from the point of view of the thought: we jump from the bridge into the wagon!

For example, as you're meditating, the thought 'I don't have time for this, I've got too much to do today,' might pop into your mind. If you believe this, you'll probably stop meditating and start working. It's strange, though, that just a few minutes previously you thought that you *did* have time to meditate, otherwise you wouldn't have sat down to do it. This illustrates an important point: our thoughts are not necessarily facts – even those that say they are!

Of course, it's not that everything we think is untrue, it's just that not everything we think is true or helpful, and mindfulness helps us to notice our thoughts without necessarily taking them as the truth, without buying into them. Instead, we notice thoughts as they arise in our mind, we see them as mental events rather than as facts, and let them go.

A way into the practice of noticing thoughts and letting them go is to practise listening to sounds. Most sounds occur independently of us: we have no control over them – planes, traffic, people talking, a neighbour's radio, hedge-trimmers, road-drills. Trying to prevent such sounds from happening would be futile and would lead to frustration. Similarly, we can't prevent thoughts from arising in our minds. What we *can* do is watch them come and go, or perhaps stick around for a while, just as sounds do.

Meditation: Listening to sounds

This works best if you are in a place where there are some sounds, otherwise it's a different practice: listening to silence! Although that is a lovely practice in itself, it won't help us to practise noticing and letting go. If you have tinnitus you may prefer to try this practice in the context of the following chapter – Working with difficult experiences.

Meditation 3: listening to sounds 🔊

Close your eyes and listen ... you don't need to make
any special effort, just listen to whatever sounds
are occurring at the moment: people walking past,
cars accelerating, a neighbour's radio, the hum of an
electrical appliance ...

Allow the sounds to come to you, not straining to hear
or trying to shut out any noises that you don't want
... just let all the sounds be present, as they are, some
perhaps coming and going, others perhaps constant ...

Maybe you notice that you get a little caught up in
some sounds: 'Who is that talking?', 'What's that
noise?', 'Why do my neighbours have to play their
music so loud?' That's OK, just notice that and, as best
you can, let them go ...

If you hear something you don't like, can you feel your resistance to it, your not-wanting-it-to-be-there? ...

Or perhaps you can hear a pleasant sound, like a bird singing or a song on a radio. Can you feel your attraction to it, a desire to focus just on this sound? ...

Can you let go of wanting and not wanting, and just be an impartial observer, simply allowing whatever sounds arise to be there? ...

Do this for five minutes or so.

Your experience

Write down your experience of listening to sounds. You may wish to consider some of the following questions.

- What did you hear?

- Did you notice some sounds and let them go?

- Did some sounds captivate you?

- Did you want some sounds to cease?

The danger of believing an untrue thought

For much of the time, buying into a thought is relatively harmless – it won't hurt us or anyone else if we stop meditating because we think we don't have time, even though that may not be true. However, some of our thoughts can cause us to suffer unnecessarily if we believe them. For instance, you might have the thought 'I've got so much to do at work, I'll never get it all done.' This may not be true, at least the second part of the statement, but if you believe it, you're likely to feel anxious and stressed and you might even lose sleep, all for no reason. Or you might be trying to do something difficult and think 'This is too hard, I can't do it.' Again, this may not be true, but if you believe it, you might give up, which may give rise to another thought: 'I'm not much good at anything' – almost definitely untrue – which may give rise to yet another thought 'I'm a failure' – definitely untrue! – which can easily lead to a state of depression.

Seeing thoughts as mental events and letting them go is not easy and it will take some practice. If you've never practised mindfulness before the chances are that you won't actually notice thoughts as they come into your mind, but will only realise them a little later; you'll jump into one of the wagons of the train and travel for a few miles before realising that's what you've done.

In that case, the practice at first will be to notice that you've already got caught in a thought, and *then* to let go of it. That's OK – the way we learn is first to notice after the event, then during the event, and then, finally, just as the thought is coming into your mind.

Let's try.

Meditation 4: mindfulness of breathing, working with thoughts

Get into a comfortable posture and close your eyes. Briefly scan the whole of your body, noticing and feeling all the sensations that are present ...

Now turn your attention to your breath, feeling the movements of the body as you breathe in and breathe out ...

Do you notice when a thought arises in your mind? Can you let go of it and come back to your breath? ...

Perhaps you only notice once the thought has arisen and you're 'in' it? If so, see if you can let go of it and come back to the breath ...

Stay with the sensations of the breath, and see if you are able to notice the next thought that arises in your mind ...

Is it easy to let go of the thought once it's arisen? If not, we'll discuss this in the next chapter ... for now, continue to notice thoughts and let them go, as best you can ...

Your experience

Write down your experience of doing this practice. You might like to consider some of the following questions.

■ Did you notice thoughts as they arose in your mind?

■ Were you able to let them go?

■ Did some thoughts take you away from the breath?

■ Did you notice that you'd been caught up in a thought and then come back to the breath?

■ Were there any thoughts that you were unable to let go of, or that kept returning?

The value of directed thinking

You may have got the impression from reading this chapter that I consider thinking to be a bad thing, or at least that it doesn't have much value – just watch thoughts and let them go. This is not the case, though; thinking can be immensely valuable if it is fully conscious and directed. Everything I've written above refers to those stray, random, distracted and semi-conscious thoughts that just arise unbidden in our minds most of the time. When we get carried away by such thoughts, we could say that we are not thinking so much as being thought – the tail is wagging the dog!

Sometimes it can be valuable to think something through, to come to a conclusion if possible, or at least to realise that a conclusion is not yet possible. For instance we may have a decision to make that requires us to think about the possible consequences of following through a certain course of action, such as, 'Shall I move house?' In trying to think this through we will probably become aware of stray, random thoughts that distract us from our task. In that case, our object of mindfulness would be the thoughts connected with the possibility of moving house; the other thoughts that 'intrude' upon this topic should be dealt with in the way that I have suggested above – simply notice them and let them go.

Meditation: Moving mindfully

The meditations that I've described up to now have been done in stillness: lying down or sitting. Now I'm going to introduce a moving meditation, consisting of a series of standing movements. Their intention is to support and encourage a sense of being grounded, relaxed and in touch with the centre and core of your body.

Throughout the movements, pay attention to the sensations in your body. Be curious about what you can feel and sense there. Notice any tension and, as best you can, let your body soften and open. Before starting the movements, and occasionally in between them, stand still for a few moments, noticing all the sensations of the body, feeling the breath and checking in with your experience. You might also like to try shaking your body every now and then, in between the movements, jiggling all your joints. Shaking is an excellent way to release the build-up of stress in our body tissues; it stimulates the flow of fluid between our joints to support greater ease and spaciousness. Animals shake naturally as a way of discharging tension after moments of heightened danger or threat.

As you explore these movements, be aware of your breathing. Don't hold the breath, but let it flow naturally, and you might like to explore exhaling through the mouth occasionally. This is another good way to release tension and connect to the breath. To do this, open your mouth a little and sigh out from the back of your throat, sounding an 'ah' or 'ha'. Let the inhale flow in through your nose and then again exhale through your mouth. This way of breathing naturally lengthens the breath and calms the body.

You can be playful with these movements. Don't go too slowly as you will become rigid. Don't go too fast as you won't be able to savour the sensations. Finally, look after yourself as you do them. Obviously, I don't know you and your body, and it could be that one or more of the movements described here are not for you. Only you know that, so listen to your body and its needs. If you have a health condition, you might want to show these movements to your doctor or physiotherapist before doing them.

Meditation 5: moving mindfully

Stand with your feet hip-width apart and parallel. Spread your feet into the floor and soften your knees so that they are slightly bent and not locked. Let your arms hang by your sides and your shoulders drop down, away from your neck and ears. Close or soften your eyes and take time to notice how your body feels. What sensations are you aware of? How is your breathing?

Keeping your knees soft and your arms hanging by your sides, gently bounce, creating a jiggling movement like shaking a bottle of water. Keep your knees and ankles soft and let the movement begin in your feet and legs and come up into your pelvis, spine, hands, arms and shoulders. You can also add in shaking movements of your arms and hands. After a while, let the movements subside and pause, feeling the after-flow of sensations.

Below is a great movement you can come back to between the other movements. It is a movement in which you can be playful – in fact it's quite hard to do it seriously!

Circle your pelvis and hips, as if you are drawing circles with them. You can rest your hands on the front or sides of your pelvis to help feel the movement. Let this movement help you to bring awareness down into the centre of your body.

Roll your shoulders, either together or one at a time, moving them backwards, downwards, forwards and upwards. Take care not to push your head and neck forwards as you move. Reverse the direction and finish with circling your shoulders backwards a few times. Keep your arms and hands relaxed and let them join in with this movement however they want to. As you move your shoulders, explore opening your mouth, relaxing your jaw and sighing out through your open mouth as you exhale. Let the movement be a self-massage for your shoulders, shoulder blades and upper back.

Gentle neck rolls: imagine that you're drawing very small circles in the air with the tip of your nose. Open your mouth slightly as you do this to encourage your jaw to soften and relax your tongue. After a while circle your nose in the other direction.

Keeping your knees soft, and initiating the movement from the centre of your body, swing from side to side. Your pelvis, spine and head will rotate together as you turn. Feel the gentle twist in your spine. Keep your feet firmly planted and only turn as far as feels natural.

Let your arms swing loose to join the movement, and let your hands tap your back at the end of each turn. Imagine your arms are like ribbons round the Maypole of your spine.

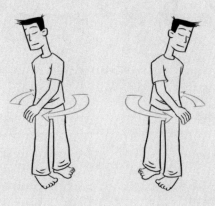

Keeping your feet firmly planted on the ground and your knees soft, extend your right arm up beside your right ear. Reach your right arm over your head to the left, allowing the elbow to bend a little as you do this. Gently arch your torso towards the left, allowing your left hand to slide down the outside of your thigh. Keep your chest and belly, and gaze, facing forwards, and the weight even on both feet as you open the right side of your body. Repeat on the other side.

You could imagine that you are like a monkey reaching up to pick a banana and give a little tug to pick the fruit as you bring your arm down. Feel the sensations in the sides of your torso as you explore this movement, how one side lengthens and the other side shortens.

Standing firmly on both feet, spread and open the soles of your feet. Take your time to shift your weight very slowly over to one foot and, very gradually, bit by bit, lift the weight off the other foot. You don't need to lift this foot high off the floor – just a little way, maybe even still resting on the tips of the toes. Can you balance and keep the rest of your body relaxed? Can you feel your breath as you balance? Play with balance and then very slowly shift your weight to the opposite side.

To complete this movement practice, stand and be still. Notice the sensations of your body and breath. Has your awareness of your body changed from when you began? If so, how? Rest in the sensations for a few moments and consciously anchor any changes you might feel.

Now, as you go about your day, see if you can bring a similar degree of awareness to the movements you make in your everyday life, such as opening a door, lifting a pen from your desk, turning on a light.

Your experience

Write down what you noticed as you did these movements, the physical sensations as well as any thoughts, feelings, emotions or judgements you had about them or yourself. You may also want to write down how you feel now, having done them.

Physical sensations: ....

....

Thoughts: ....

....

Feelings: ....

....

Judgements: ....

....

Taking a break from activity

How many times a day do you stop whatever it is you're doing and take a break? *Really* take a break, as in do nothing for a little while? It's fine to have a full life, but a life of constant activity isn't good for us, it keeps us locked in doing mode and is one of the causes of anxiety and stress, not to mention irritability.

I invite you to take a break – in fact, take many breaks throughout your day. They don't have to be long breaks – you don't have to take a 15-minute tea break, although that would be great – it can be just for a minute, or even for just a few breaths. Added together these breaks might come to ten or fifteen minutes. Can you spare that much time in your busy schedule? If not, you may need to ask yourself whether your lifestyle is good for you in the long run. When we are constantly on the go we tend to get frazzled, our minds get tired, and we end up paying less attention to the task in hand. Consequently, we don't do as good a job as we're capable of. Perhaps taking regular breaks is, in the end, more efficient.

Mindfulness in action 3: take a break

Stop whatever you're doing a number of times a day.

Here are some ideas that might help you to do that:

Give yourself permission. It's interesting that when I ask people to do nothing for a few minutes in my workshops, people often say, 'It was great to be given permission to do nothing'! So, give yourself permission to do nothing, to take a break from activity, a number of times a day.

Don't do anything else. Let go completely of what you've been doing, really let yourself have a break. Stop doing, stop being productive or useful, be useless for a little while. Rest in being mode.

Have a holiday from doing mode. Having a break means shifting from doing to being mode for a little while.

When we're in being mode we're simply being here, in the moment, fully present, relaxed but alert, appreciating the richness of the present moment, even with its imperfections and problems.

Take lots of micro-breaks. If you don't feel you have the time to take a five- or ten-minute break, take lots of tiny breaks: close your eyes and follow your breath for three breaths, look out of the window for 30 seconds, stand up if you've been sitting, sit down if you've been standing or walking.

Change your activity. If you've been doing one thing for the last hour or so, do something else for a while. Sometimes we can be grinding away at something, and it can be a relief to do something else. 'A change is as good as a rest.'

Get away from technology. If you work with a computer, walk away from it for a little while, turn off your phone, or at least don't answer it. We used to live without these things. Now we tend to be tyrannised by them.

Get into your body. If you're doing some mental work, such as writing or working with a computer, do something with your body. Stand up, stretch, go for a micro-walk, lie down, or simply close your eyes and notice the sensations in your body; the feeling of the soles of your feet on the floor, your hands resting in your lap, your breath flowing in and out.

Summary

In this chapter I've introduced the idea that thoughts are not necessarily facts and that, once you become aware that thoughts are simply that – just thoughts – you have the opportunity to let them go if you want to.

Practice

To support you in this I've introduced the meditation practice of listening to sounds, and the mindfulness of breathing with a particular emphasis on noticing thoughts and letting them go.

Practise both of these meditations a few times, but don't forget the body scan. I've also invited you to take a break from activity every now and then. Do that as well as continuing to do a routine activity mindfully, and doing something slowly.

 To download the template of a journal for this chapter's practice go to www.breathworks-mindfulness.org.uk/the-little-mindfulness-workbook.

5 Working with difficult experiences

Idea: Experiencing your experience

You'll probably have noticed that letting go of a thought is made more or less difficult by the kind of thought you're having. Some thoughts have a strong emotional charge to them and these can be very difficult to let go.

Let's say that you had an unpleasant row with someone you love this morning. He said a number of hurtful things to you and you retaliated with a few home truths. Now you're feeling quite stirred up, hurt, guilty about some of the things you said and a bit nervous about seeing him again later today. If you sit down to meditate on your breath, what do you think is going to happen? No doubt you'll think about the row, playing it over and over in your mind, now feeling the hurt, the injustice of some of the things he said, now feeling angry and coming up with things you wished you'd said, now feeling nervous about when you see him this evening. So, you take your awareness to your breath. How long do you think you'll be able to stay with the breath before thoughts of the row break in? Three seconds maybe? Now, you replay something he said and feel hurt and angry for a little while, then go back to the breath. Three seconds later you've suddenly thought about something else you should have said. That keeps you busy for a few minutes before you realise what you're doing. Ah. Back to the breath, and so on, the breath – the row – the breath – the row – the breath ...

The thing is, your feelings about the row are calling for your attention. You'd have to be a robot to be able to just forget it and pay attention to your breath. (Of course, a robot wouldn't have had a row in the first place, but that's another matter.) They're calling for attention because your relationship with your loved one matters to you. You're hurting and troubled and you need to attend to that. What we usually do, though, is pay attention to the *thoughts* about the argument – what he said, what you said, what you should have said, what you'll say when you see him this evening, what you hope he'll say, etc. In mindfulness practice we go underneath the thoughts, as it were, to the feelings and emotions, and allow ourselves to feel them fully. Where do we feel them? In the body. As you sit there, allowing yourself to feel, see if you can locate them in your body.

Now, rather than trying to prise your mind away from the row, the feelings and emotions evoked by the row *become your meditation*. You can breathe with those feelings. Breathing in and out with the anger, the hurt, the regret and so on. That's all you need to do.

Not all charged thoughts are unpleasant of course. If you are getting married in a couple of days time, or going on holiday tomorrow morning, when you sit down to meditate, thoughts about the wedding or the holiday will probably arise because you're happy and excited. With positive experiences you can do the same as I suggested for the negative experience: try not to get caught up in the thoughts about the wedding or the holiday – planning, worrying, remembering to phone the caterers – rather feel the excitement, the happiness of the occasion, and meditate with that.

Meditation: Mindfulness of breathing, working with a charged thought

You can only do this practice – indeed the only time you *need* to do it – is when you have a charged thought. On the whole, when we meditate, we first work with our thoughts in the way described in Chapter 4, but if we notice that one or more of our thoughts are charged with emotion we can do the following.

Meditation 6: mindfulness of breathing, working with a charged thought

Get into a comfortable posture and close your eyes. Briefly scan the whole of your body, noticing and feeling all the sensations that are present ... Then turn your attention to the breath, feeling the movements of the body as you breathe in and breathe out ...

Notice any thoughts that arise in your mind, and as best you can, let them go ...

If a thought comes back a number of times, the chances are it has an emotional charge. Just check that out. Is that the case? ... If so, take your attention to the emotion that's driving it ... You don't need to identify that emotion, no need to give it a label, it's enough to feel it ...

Where do you feel it? Can you locate it somewhere in your body? ... Can you allow it to be fully present, fully felt? ...

It may help if you breathe with the emotion, to breathe into it on the in breath, and see if you can let go of any resistance to it on the out breath ...

Continue to do this for a few minutes, allowing yourself to feel the emotion(s), and then bring the practice to a close.

Your experience

Write down your experience of this practice. If there was a charged thought, were you able to 'go underneath' it and feel the emotional charge? What was this like? Could you locate that emotion somewhere in your body?

What was the thought? ....

What was the emotion, or emotions, that were 'driving' the thought?

....

Were you able to locate where in your body you felt the emotion(s)?

....

Idea: The paradox of mindfulness

Obviously you're reading this book and doing the practices because you're hoping to achieve something. You want to get from where you currently are (let's call that A) to another, better state (let's call that B).

A ————————————▶ B

How do we achieve that? At the heart of mindfulness practice lies a paradox: if you want to get from A to B, you have to really be at A! Let's say you want to get from a state of anxiety to a state of calm. Have you ever tried not to feel anxious when you're feeling anxious? If so, how did it go? Not very well, I suspect. What we resist tends to persist. Our very efforts not to have an experience keep us tied to it. So, rather than making efforts to stop feeling anxious and start feeling calm, we simply need to feel the anxiety, explore the feelings, be curious about them. Where do you feel the anxiety in your body? How does it actually feel?

A   B

Simply bringing awareness to unpleasant or difficult experiences changes the experience, even if only slightly. When we bring awareness to a situation, we also bring a certain amount of calm to it. Rather than trying to get to B, B comes to us, simply through the act of being mindful.

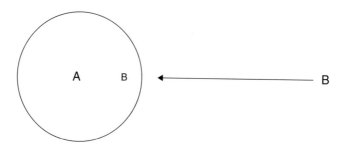

Returning to our theme of *doing* and *being*, instead of enlisting our doing mode of mind to fix the problem of anxiety, we simply 'be' with the anxiety. Be careful though – A – in this case, anxiety – is not the secondary experience. It's not all the thoughts, emotions, judgements, analysing and problem-solving that usually accompany our feelings of anxiety. A is the primary experience – our direct, felt experience.

At first you may not notice the calming effect that mindfulness has, especially when your primary experience (anxiety or whatever) is very intense. But if you pay attention especially *to your awareness* of the anxiety, you'll notice a small oasis of calm in the midst of the storm. As you practise, this little oasis will grow, and with more practice it will become bigger than the anxiety.

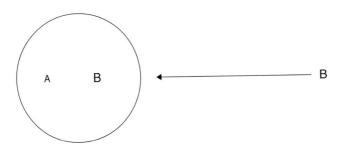

Notice that, although you've now brought B (calm) to your experience of A (anxiety), A is still there. You're now experiencing your anxiety in a calmer way, but you want to get rid of the anxiety altogether, right? With continued practice of mindfulness, with more experience of being mode, you'll strengthen the state of calm, causing the anxiety to gradually diminish.

We don't want to get rid of anxiety altogether though, because, as we'll see in Chapter 6, anxiety has a purpose – to protect us from harm. Anxiety is only problematic when it overworks, causing us to feel anxious when there is really no need. What we're aiming for is to feel anxiety only when it's appropriate to feel it; that is, when we really are in some kind of danger.

Acceptance

Whatever our A is, when we stop resisting it, stop trying to push it away, stop trying to not have it, and instead allow it simply to be as it is, we find that, in time, the feelings subside and calm down. 'In time' could be a lot of time though – there are no quick fixes in mindfulness work. In the meantime, we can hold our anxiety, or whatever our A happens to be – our primary experience – calmly, accepting that that's the way things are right now. Accepting really means accepting. If we 'accept' an unpleasant experience so that it will go away, we're not really accepting it, we're bargaining with it: 'I'll let you stay for a little while as long as you go soon!' Really being at A means *really* being at A.

Acceptance doesn't mean merely putting up with, or resignation, or stoic endurance. Acceptance comes from the Latin *acceptare*, which means 'take or receive willingly', so it's a positive, active state, not a passive, negative one. We could say it's the willingness to have our experience.

Meditation: Being with unwanted experience

In this meditation practice we're going to have a go at being with something that's going on in our life at the moment that we don't like. It could be a relationship difficulty; perhaps you're having a conflict with someone right now. It could be that work is particularly difficult right now. It could be a financial problem, or a health issue. You can choose any kind of difficulty for this practice, although it's best to choose something that's not too distressing to begin with. Try practising on something relatively easy to work with and then, as you get the hang of it, you can choose something more difficult. As you'll see, I've included physical pain and other kinds of physical discomfort; you can work with any unwanted experience at all.

Meditation 7: being with unwanted experience

Get into as comfortable a posture as you can. Close your eyes and allow your awareness to sink down into your body ... Scan your whole body briefly, to get a sense of the whole of it ...

As best you can, give yourself up to the gentle pull of gravity, allowing it to pull you down towards the earth ... notice if you're resisting gravity in some way, and if you are, see if you can let go of that resistance ...

Now rest your awareness on the feelings of the breath entering and leaving your body ... allow the rhythm of your breath to soothe you ...

Now, bring to mind something that's happening in your life that you don't want to be happening ... what does it feel like? ...

Does your mind start to get busy, arguing, struggling, looking for a way out? If so, see if you can let go of the urge to think about it, to try to solve it, and instead, allow yourself simply to feel it ...

Can you locate that feeling in your body? ... If you're able to do this, see if you can just be with that feeling, exploring it, being curious about it ...

If the unwanted experience is physical pain or discomfort, gently take your awareness there and let it rest on that discomfort, just as it did on the feelings of the breath ...

Explore the sensations of the pain or discomfort ... What are they actually like? ... Are they constant or do they change? ... Are they hard and solid, or are they softer? ... Can you *lean into* the pain, much as you might lean into a strong wind that you're walking into?

Or it could be that you have some other unpleasant physical experience, such as tinnitus, fatigue, whatever ... see if you can simply be with whatever it is you're experiencing ...

If the experience becomes too intense you can always back off and take your awareness somewhere else, such as the sensations of the breath ...

You may also find that you have a strong resistance to being so close to the experience, in which case you could try leaning into the resistance itself ... what does resistance feel like? ...

You may find it useful to imagine that you're breathing into the experience on the in breath ... and then have a sense of letting go on the out breath ... not letting go of the experience, but of your resistance to it ...

What I'm asking you to do is hard, and you may be gritting your teeth, as it were, with determination ... If so, perhaps you could allow yourself to soften a little, recognise what a hard thing it is that you're doing, and bring in some kindness towards yourself ... a softness, a gentleness, as you might if a small child you were looking after fell over and grazed their knee ... they are on the ground, upset, hurting ... what would you do? Probably you'd hold them in your arms, which would enable them to feel the pain and upset more easily, held with love and compassion ... can you have this same attitude towards yourself? ...

Now broaden your awareness, becoming aware once again of the whole of your body ... and your breath ... and the room that you're in ... and when you're ready, open your eyes.

Your experience

Write down your experience of doing this practice.

What was the unwanted experience? ....

What was it like to be with this experience? ....

Did any thoughts arise in connection with the experience? If so, what were they?

....

Were you able to let go of those thoughts and come back to the primary experience?

....

Were you able to bring a sense of kindness to your experience?

....

Things we can't change

There are some aspects of our experience that we can't change, of course. You may not like the British weather for instance, and 'really being with it' won't turn it into a tropical paradise. More seriously, if your A is chronic physical pain, simply being at A is not going to take you to a pain-free B. Accepting such intractable situations really does mean accepting them. This may seem rather bleak and hopeless. However, if we return to the idea of primary and secondary experience, from Chapter 2, we'll recall that much of our suffering comes about because we resist and struggle against unpleasant experience. If we can let go of that resistance – the unhelpful thoughts, negative emotions and harsh judgements – then our primary experience becomes easier to bear. This is partly because there is simply less suffering to deal with, but in addition, many people find that letting go of their resistance to unpleasant experience alleviates it. Our experience of pain, in fact any unpleasant experience, is strongly influenced by our state of mind. It simply feels worse when we fight it.

Accept a difficult situation

Now we're going to see if we can be with a difficult situation, as it's actually happening, and accept it rather than fight against it. It's best to start practising with something relatively mild, such as being caught in a traffic jam or stuck on a late train, having to do something you'd rather not have to do, feeling irritated with someone's behaviour, getting caught in the rain (assuming you don't like rain). Once you've had some practice in being with relatively mild experiences you can move on to more difficult ones.

Mindfulness in action 4: accepting a difficult experience

Next time you find yourself in a stressful, unpleasant or difficult situation, first of all, simply notice that it's happening and that *it's unpleasant*. Where do you feel the unpleasantness? In your head, stomach, chest, arms or legs? Or somewhere else? See if you can *be with the unpleasant sensations* without reacting.

Acknowledge that it's difficult, that it's an experience of suffering. You might even say to yourself 'This is a moment of suffering.' Try not to beat yourself up about it, but instead treat yourself as you would a friend or loved one who is having a hard time. Kindly, considerately, gently. After all, you're doing something difficult.

Using the breath can help. Take your attention to it, especially as you feel it lower down in your body. Feel your abdomen swelling and subsiding. You can imagine *breathing into* the unpleasant experience and, on the out breath, see if you can let go of your resistance to what's happening.

See if you can *allow* the difficult situation to simply be there, just as it is, without you needing to do anything about it. See if you can hold it in your attention, in a soft, gentle, calm way. Breathing in the experience, breathing out the resistance. Breathing in the discomfort, breathing out kindness to yourself.

Summary

This chapter has been all about being with difficult, unpleasant, even painful experiences – learning to accept rather than resist them. We've seen that, paradoxically, when we simply allow an experience to be present, without fighting or resisting it, it tends to change. Not that it necessarily 'goes away', but by bringing awareness to our experience we also bring a sense of spaciousness and calm, which subtly changes it.

Practice

To help you bring these ideas into your life, in this chapter I've introduced two new meditations: mindfulness of breathing – working with a 'charged' thought, and being with an unwanted experience. Actually these are not so much new meditations as specific ways of working with difficult experiences in meditation. That is, you only need do them when you *have* a charged thought or an unwanted experience. However, it's worth practising with relatively minor difficulties now, such as a sore knee or a feeling of slight anxiety, so that you can draw on this experience when you *are* dealing with a major stressor. I've also introduced a new *mindfulness in action*: accepting a difficult experience.

To download the template of a journal for this chapter's practice go to www.breathworks-mindfulness.org.uk/the-little-mindfulness-workbook.

6 Noticing the good things

Idea: Balancing the Negativity Bias

In the last chapter we focused on difficult experiences and learned how to work mindfully with them. Now we have to be a little careful. No doubt we all have difficulties in life, and learning how to be with them without reacting means that we won't add extra unnecessary suffering to our experience, but good things happen too, and it's easy to overlook them. To be mindful is to pay attention to whatever happens to be occurring in the moment, but there are many things we could attend to, and *what* we pay attention to determines, to some extent, our experience.

Let's say that when you wake up you think about the various things you have to do today. You have a number of tasks, one of which is to give someone some bad news, and you suspect they'll take it badly. In fact, you're a little afraid that they'll become angry with you.

If you're like me (and, I suspect, most people), the thought of that task will loom larger in your mind than all the other things you have to do. This is because we have what neuro-psychologists call a negativity bias in the brain, a strong tendency to notice and dwell on negative events and experiences. There is an evolutionary reason for this. Our cave-dwelling ancestors were vulnerable to attack by predators and hostile tribes, not to mention disease, starvation, etc., so in order to survive they had to be hyper-vigilant to threats. They had to look out for danger before they looked for opportunities, because if they missed the piece of fruit hanging from the tree, they'd go hungry for a while, whereas if they didn't notice the tiger hiding in the bushes ...

We've inherited this negativity bias, which means that we notice the bad things before we notice anything good; we operate on the principle *better safe than sorry*. While this works well from the point of view of our survival, it doesn't help us to enjoy a sense of well-being, tranquillity and happiness. It's hard to relax and enjoy yourself when you're looking out for potential dangers. Imagine trying to have a good time at a party if you felt that someone there wanted to harm you, or having a swim in the sea if you suspected there were sharks lurking nearby!

Our brain evolved in the way it did to make sure we survived, not to make us happy. So we need to work against this negativity bias, which we do by turning our attention to the positive – the good things that happen, the pleasant experiences. This is not looking at the world through rose-tinted glasses or 'thinking positive'; it means getting a more balanced view – a truer view – of our situation. Don't worry, when danger threatens you will still notice it and be able to react appropriately, you just won't be so hyper-vigilant and wary all the time.

Enquiry 3: seeking out the pleasant

Spend some time looking around you for things you find pleasant. Use all of your senses – sight, sound, smell, touch, taste. It could be the colour of a wall, the smell of a flower, the feel of a cushion. When you find something, stay with it for a little while and relish the pleasure. Notice how you experience the pleasure. Where do you feel it? Let's say you're enjoying looking at the sky: where is the pleasure in that experience? Is it just in the eyes, or do you feel the enjoyment of it elsewhere, such as the heart area, or the stomach? Similarly, if you're enjoying the aroma of coffee, is the pleasure just in the nose, or do you feel it somewhere else too?

Your experience

Write down your experience of seeking out the pleasant.

What things gave you pleasure?

....

Try to describe the pleasure you felt for each.

....

Which senses were involved?

....

How do you feel now as you write about your experience?

....

As well as *noticing* the negative more readily than we do the positive, we tend to *remember* unpleasant experiences more than we do pleasant ones. Negative experiences go straight into our implicit memory while positive experiences take a little while to do this. (Implicit memory stores experiences, skills, etc., while explicit memory stores facts, ideas, etc.) As the neuro-psychologist Rick Hanson puts it, negative experiences are like Velcro – they stick, while positive experiences are like Teflon – they slide off us. There's an evolutionary reason for this too: for our cave-dwelling forbears, negative experiences were often dangerous, and it was more important to learn from them than it was to learn from positive experiences. This means that when we look back on the day, the week, the year, we'll tend to remember the difficult and unpleasant experiences more readily than we'll remember the good ones.

So far I've been discussing sense pleasures, but there are of course other kinds of pleasure. One of these is called value-based pleasure, which is the enjoyment we derive from doing things that are meaningful to us: the satisfaction of doing a job well, the quiet joy of a generous act, the warm feeling of helping someone in a difficult situation, the excited feeling of success when you reach a goal you've been aiming at for some time. These kinds of experience can go unnoticed too. We'll explore these kinds of pleasures in a little more detail in the next chapter, but for now I'm going to introduce a practice that enables us to notice *all* of the good things as they occur and then to stay with them for a little while, allowing them to enter our implicit memory.

Mindfulness in action 5: letting in the good

This is a practice that Rick Hanson developed. It has three parts.

1. **Notice a positive experience**

This will probably be something quite ordinary, such as someone smiling at you briefly as they pass, the sun shining on your desk as you work, the feeling of satisfaction in doing a good job. Most positive experiences are quite ordinary and relatively minor, but they are still real. We have many of these experiences every day, but they often come and go unnoticed.

Now, allow yourself to feel the pleasure of it. Let yourself feel good about it. Let it affect you.

Notice any reluctance you might feel to doing this: perhaps a sense that you don't have time, or that you don't deserve it, or that it's self-indulgent, or that if you allowed yourself to enjoy the pleasure of these small things, you'd somehow let your guard down and allow bad things to happen.

Then turn back towards the positive experience; keep opening to it, breathing into it, enjoying it.

2. **Stay with the experience**

Now stay with the experience for 10, 20, even 30 seconds. If you get distracted by something else, simply return to the experience. Allow yourself to really enjoy it. Soften and open around the experience; let it fill your mind; give over to it in your body.

The longer you keep it in your awareness and the more emotionally stimulating it is, the stronger the trace in implicit memory.

3. **Absorb the experience**

Now allow the experience to sink into you. You do this simply by staying with the experience and allowing yourself to feel it. Rather as you might on a cold day when the sun suddenly comes out, and you allow the sun to warm the whole of you, inside as well as out. Or if you were to drink a cup of hot chocolate on a cold wintry day, and you feel the warmth spread through you.

Do this a number of times a day. It doesn't take long – 10, 20 seconds each time. Doing this practice helps to change the brain, building neural pathways that enable us to notice and remember the good things in life more readily.

Summary

In this chapter we've been considering the brain's inbuilt negativity bias, working against this by paying attention to the good things that happen. Although this is a short chapter, it's no less important than the others. In fact, many of my students report that the practice of noticing the good had a bigger effect than anything else they learned. Sometimes small is beautiful!

Practice

I haven't introduced a new meditation practice in this chapter, but I suggest that you do the body scan and mindfulness of breathing with a focus on noticing the pleasant sensations in the body. You don't have to ignore or try to distract yourself from any unpleasant sensations in your experience. Allow them to be there too, but notice and dwell on the pleasant. The *mindfulness in action* is to let in the good.

 To download the template of a journal for this chapter's practice go to www.breathworks-mindfulness.org.uk/the-little-mindfulness-workbook.

7

Kindfulness

Idea: The three major emotion systems

In the last chapter we saw that *what* we pay attention to is important. In this chapter we're going to consider *how* we pay attention, the *quality* of our attending. The word attention has two principal meanings: it means to focus the mind on something, and it means to care for. We've looked mainly at the first of these so far, although we touched on the second in the practices in which we worked with difficult experiences, bringing in a gentle, kindly attitude to them. In this chapter we're going to explore this dimension of mindfulness a little further.

A model of our emotional lifestyle

A helpful framework for understanding emotions is one that comes from evolutionary neuroscience, which the psychologist Paul Gilbert has helpfully simplified for us. This framework divides emotions into three categories, called emotion regulation systems. These are:

1. The Self Protection, or Threat, System
2. The Resource-seeking, or Drive, System
3. The Contentment, or Soothing, System.

In Chapter 2, you may remember, I made a distinction between feelings and emotions, and although what we're currently exploring are called *emotion* regulation systems, they include both emotions *and* feelings. Gilbert gives each system a colour, and I'll now refer to each system by that colour: the Self Protection system is *red*, the Drive system is *blue*, and the Contentment system is *green*.

The three emotion systems[1]

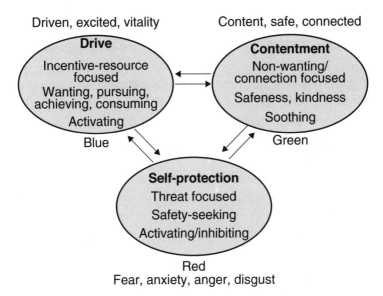

Driven, excited, vitality

Drive
Incentive-resource focused
Wanting, pursuing, achieving, consuming
Activating

Blue

Content, safe, connected

Contentment
Non-wanting/ connection focused
Safeness, kindness
Soothing

Green

Self-protection
Threat focused
Safety-seeking
Activating/inhibiting

Red
Fear, anxiety, anger, disgust

---

1 Slightly adapted from Paul Gilbert, *The Compassionate Mind*, (2009, London: Constable and Robinson), p. 22. Used with permission.

The red system - self-protection

The function of these emotions is to notice when we're in danger and to activate us to protect ourselves and those we care for. These emotions include fear, anxiety, anger and disgust. (If we open the fridge door and we smell an unpleasant odour, the disgust we experience protects us from the danger of consuming something that could make us ill or even kill us.) Interestingly, all the emotions in this system are unpleasant, which shows us that not everything unpleasant is 'bad' or undesirable: if there was a fire in your building, you'd be right to feel afraid and to leave the building as quickly as possible. This emotion system is connected with one of the oldest parts of our brain, the *amygdala*, which is situated at the base of the skull. When we feel threatened, hormones such as *adrenalin* and *cortisol* are released into our bloodstream, which give us a boost of energy that helps us to respond rapidly: to escape, fight or hide.

The red system is connected with the negativity bias that we explored in the previous chapter. When we're on the lookout for danger we're operating in this emotion system and, as we've seen, the brain gives more priority to dealing with threats than it does to opportunities. This means that we can get stuck in the red system, even when we're not in danger, and although bursts of adrenalin and cortisol are fine for short periods, over longer periods they have a bad effect on our health, including a weakening of our immune system.

The blue system - drive

There are two dimensions to this system: first, it motivates us to seek and get the good things in life, and second, when we get those things, we're rewarded by feeling good. This is due to a neurotransmitter called *dopamine*, which gives us the motivation to pursue our goals and, when we achieve them, activates the brain's reward system to give us a flush of pleasure. For this reason, some people call dopamine the reward chemical. The emotions in this system include desire (to get the good things), excitement (as we get closer to capturing them), joy and pleasure (when we get them).

The blue system is connected to the red, in that, if something or someone prevents us from obtaining what we're pursuing, we may become frustrated and perhaps angry. At those times both emotion systems are activated simultaneously.

This is one of the reasons why it's not a good idea to base our happiness on achieving goals and obtaining things, because we don't always get what we want. There's another reason, too. Because dopamine feels good we'll want to repeat the experience, and if the blue system is not balanced by the green (see below), then as soon as we get one thing we start seeking another, never satisfied with what we've got. Some people are particularly reward-sensitive, and these people are more susceptible to addiction.

The green system - contentment

This is activated when we feel safe and when we don't want or need anything. The feelings in this system include contentment, a feeling of safeness, peacefulness and fulfilment, as well as emotions that connect us positively to others: kindness, affection, appreciation, gratitude, love, compassion, etc. For this reason, it's also called the calm-and-connect system. The chemicals involved in this system include the *endorphins* and *oxytocin*, the latter of which is popularly known as the love hormone. When endorphins and oxytocin are released, we experience a strong sense of well-being. In fact, some endorphins are natural 'painkillers', so stimulating the green system can reduce our pain and other unpleasant physical sensations.

I've mentioned the downsides of both the red and blue systems, and there's a downside to the green too: if we spend too long there we can become apathetic, lazy and unmotivated, which leads to a loss of energy and a lowering of mood, leading eventually to depression.

The green system is not necessarily a passive state though. Being kind to someone, for instance, is active, but it's a different sort of activity from that of the blue system. When we're helping someone out, being affectionate to someone we love, being playful, we're not trying to achieve any particular goal or outcome. The help we're giving, the affection and the playfulness are their own reward.

Which emotion system do you spend most time in?

Recall the last few days and write down in the relevant oval when a certain emotion system was activated in you. For instance, in the threat oval, you might write, 'Feeling nervous about going to a meeting', or in the contentment oval you might write 'Hanging out with a friend'.

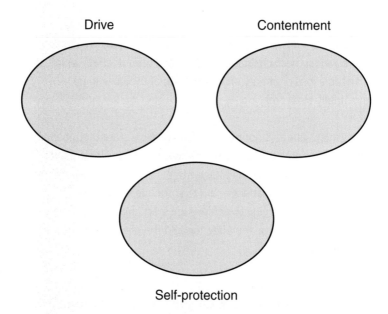

Drive

Contentment

Self-protection

Turning down the red and blue, turning up the green

The red and blue emotion systems are both about changing the current state of things – from danger to safety, and from not having to having – so they are connected with the *doing* mode of mind. The green system involves an experience of *being* – not striving after anything, but being comfortable in the present moment, just as it is.

Each of the systems has an upside and a downside, and each one needs to be regulated or balanced by the other two. That's what the arrows in between the ovals in the diagram on page 123 signify. For instance, you may be working hard to gain promotion (blue), but you also need to stop striving sometimes – to rest and be with your friends and family (green). While you're enjoying playing ball with your children (blue/green), you'll also be making sure they don't run out into the road (red).

Contemporary society values the red and blue systems much more than it does the green, and most of us need to balance this by 'turning up the green' and 'turning down the red and blue'. All the practices you've learned in this book will help you to do that. In this and the next chapter we're going to focus particularly on the connection/affection/kindness aspect of the green system.

Meditation: Kindness to self

If we want to connect positively with other people it helps if we have a positive attitude towards ourselves, and this meditation helps us to do that. You may not experience its effect immediately, in fact you probably won't. As you've probably gathered from your mindfulness practice so far, we're not looking for instant results. Think of it as sowing seeds that will grow in the future, if you nurture them. Remember that we're 'turning up the green' in this practice, not the blue! So striving, working hard, making great efforts to achieve a particular outcome doesn't work – you'll probably get frustrated if you do that and inadvertently turn up the red instead!

There are different ways of doing this practice, and I've discovered in my teaching that while one way suits some people very well, it doesn't work at all well for others. So when I'm introducing this meditation I teach three different methods using phrases, imagery and the breath. There's not enough space in this book to describe them separately, so I'm including all three in the following meditation. Have a go at all three and then choose the way that works best for you.

Meditation 8: kindness to self

Sit in a comfortable and upright posture, close your eyes and spend some time just being aware of the various sensations in your body ...

Now rest your awareness on your breath, as you have done in the mindfulness of breathing ...

After a few minutes, take your awareness to your heart area, and just 'check in' how you feel right now ...

Using phrases:

Now say to yourself, 'May I be well' ... Wait a little while for that phrase to affect you ...

After a few moments repeat that phrase ...

Now try another one, 'May I be happy' ... Just say it and see what happens, if anything ...

Notice any thoughts or feelings you have in response to the phrase – perhaps 'I don't deserve to be happy' or 'I'll never be happy' or 'This is a silly thing to be doing'. Whatever thoughts may come into your mind, just remember your mindfulness training – they are just thoughts, you don't have to believe them, just let them go and continue with the practice ...

You might try other phrases, such as 'May I be free from suffering' ... 'May things go well for me' ... 'May I feel safe and secure' ... 'May I develop my potential' ... . Or you can make up your own phrases, ones that express more specifically what you want for yourself ...

Using imagery:

Imagine a warm sun ... perhaps at the end of a hot summer's day, when the sun is just above the horizon ... perhaps it's a golden colour, or maybe a deep red ... and it's radiating a soft warmth ... don't worry if you can't see it very clearly, it's OK just to get a sense of it being there ...

Now imagine that the sun is in your heart ... again, you don't need to *see* it there, just get a feeling for it ... imagine that soft, warm rays of light are radiating from it, filling your whole body with warm light ...

Imagine that this warm light is kindness ... filling your whole body ...

Using the breath:

Rest your awareness on the feelings of your breath ... breath coming in ... breath going out ...

Now imagine that the air all around you is suffused with kindness ... . (This isn't a metaphysical statement! I'm not saying that air *is* suffused with kindness – just asking you to *imagine* that it is.) So when you breathe in, you're breathing in kindness ... and when you breathe out, that kindness is permeating your whole body ...

After some time doing this, broaden your awareness to the whole of your body ... and sounds ... and then open your eyes.

Your experience

Write down your experience of doing this practice.

What happened when you used the phrases?

....

What happened when you imagined the warm sun?

....

What happened when you imagined breathing in kindness?

....

Any other comments

....

Self-criticism and self-kindness

Perhaps you think that all this talk of being kind to oneself is weak and self-indulgent. Maybe you think that being hard on yourself is the way to go, that being self-critical keeps you up to the mark, stops you from being lazy and selfish, and helps you to improve?

In fact, a couple of recent research studies suggest that the opposite is true. In these studies, people who practised self-kindness meditation were better able to acknowledge their mistakes, imperfections and negative actions, to learn from them and to change for the better, than those who hadn't done so. This is because having a positive attitude towards themselves allowed them to admit to their failings without being overwhelmed by negative emotions. Self-kindness, rather than making us weak and self-indulgent, makes us more emotionally robust and less selfish.

When we're criticised, the red system is activated in us; the criticism is felt as a threat, even if it's meant to be helpful. Similarly, when we're critical of ourselves we turn up the red, so if we're habitually self-critical then we're constantly activating the emotions of fear, anxiety and anger (directed at ourselves), and perhaps self-disgust. These emotions don't help us to become better, they just make us feel bad.

Mindfulness in action 6: spend some time in the green circle

The feelings and emotions in the green system include contentment, serenity, satisfaction, equanimity, appreciation, wonder, affection, empathy, kindness, love and compassion. It also includes the experiences of being absorbed in an activity: relaxation, fun and playfulness. The green system is where creativity most commonly occurs, because it allows us to step out of habitual ways of reacting to things and people, and to look at them afresh.

So I invite you to spend some time in the green circle every day. There are so many ways of doing this; here are just a few examples:

Stop every now and then and appreciate the world around you – the sky perhaps, or a bowl of fruit, the colour of the tie that someone's wearing.

When you're talking to someone – a friend, family member, colleague, stranger – try to connect with them as another human being; give them your whole attention; really listen to them; be interested in what they're saying.

Have some fun. This could be taking time out of your day to do a specific fun activity, or it could be just making sure you have some fun in your ordinary daily activities. Be playful. Take things a little less seriously.

Do something that absorbs your attention. Something that makes you concentrate on a task to the exclusion of all other concerns: something that causes you to be in the present moment. This could be a work task or something that you'd do at home or elsewhere. This is why people have hobbies!

Commit random acts of kindness! Do something nice for someone. Buy the *Big Issue* from a licensed seller and, if you have the time, stop and chat to them for a while. Offer to make tea for someone who seems to be under some pressure. Buy a small gift for someone you like or love. The effect of such small acts of kindness can be amazing!

Spend some time with a friend.

Go to the gym and make sure you give yourself plenty of time to enjoy the sauna, jacuzzi and shower after your workout.

Tell someone you love that you love them.

There are a thousand other ways of turning up the green, so don't confine yourself to the above examples. Be creative! Enjoy yourself.

Summary

In this chapter I've introduced the three major emotion systems, which keep us safe from harm, motivate us to get the good things in life, and allow us to rest and to connect with those around us. While all three systems are important, in our society the soothing system tends to be neglected, and mindfulness – and therefore everything you've learned and practised in this book – helps us to activate that system.

Practice

I've introduced a new meditation practice, too – kindness to self – which helps to cultivate emotional positivity and resilience. Do the kindness-to-self meditation every day, after a period of the body scan or mindfulness of breathing. The *mindfulness in action* is to spend some time in the green circle every day.

 To download the template of a journal for this chapter's practice go to www.breathworks-mindfulness.org.uk/the-little-mindfulness-workbook.

8 The social dimension of mindfulness

Idea: Mindfulness of other people

So far, our practice of mindfulness has been focused on our self and our own experience, but most of us interact in various ways with other people, so for our mindfulness practice to be complete, we need to include them. What might that mean? Let's summarise what we've learned up to this point, then we'll be in a better position to answer that question.

We've seen that mindfulness is the gentle but persistent effort to pay attention to whatever our experience is in the present moment, that it's a non-judgemental awareness; it doesn't divide experience into two separate categories and then accept one and reject the other. Rather, it's curious about everything. To be mindful is to respond to unpleasant, unwanted experiences with awareness and wisdom rather than reacting in habitual ways to them, while at the same time being aware of the brain's inbuilt negativity bias, so that we don't focus mainly on threats and faults, but remember to notice the good things, too. Finally, mindfulness is a warm, gentle, kindly, friendly awareness. To be mindful of other people, then, is to regard them in these ways.

Of course there's a big difference between a person and an inanimate object: people are not only objects but subjects too. That is, they have inner lives – they have their own awareness, their own sense of being a self, which includes feelings and emotions, thoughts, plans, ambitions, loves, fears, etc. To be mindful of other people, then, includes an awareness of them not only as objects but also as subjects, which means feeling for and respecting, or at least taking into account, their feelings, points of view, desires, etc. It means, in a word, empathising with them. It's probably true to say that everyone wants to avoid suffering and to be happy, so being mindful of others includes wishing that for them.

We've spent some time developing self-kindness; now we're going to broaden our awareness to include other people within our circle of kindness. We do that in much the same way that we did the self-kindness meditations, except that now we direct our positive feelings towards others. Let's begin with a friend or someone you care for. It's best not to choose someone you are sexually attracted to, or someone who has died, because you may then stimulate other feelings, which will tend to complicate the practice.

Meditation 9: kindness towards someone you like

Sit in a comfortable posture, close your eyes and spend some time just being aware of the various sensations in your body ...

Then rest your awareness on your breath ...

After a few minutes, take your awareness to your heart area, and just 'check in' how you feel ...

Now choose someone you like, care for or love. There may be a number of people you could choose, but don't get caught up in trying to decide – you'll have the opportunity to choose others in the next few days ...

If you're good at visualising, you'll be able to see them in your mind's eye, but don't worry if you are not so good at this – it's not important to 'see' them, just get a sense of them ... You might call to mind their name, or their voice or one of their characteristics ...

Because you like them you'll probably already have good feelings towards them, and all you have to do is dwell on those feelings, allowing them to grow ...

You can use your imagination, just as in the first stage. If you liked using the phrases in the Kindness-to-Self Meditation, you can adapt them to your friend – e.g. 'May he or she be well,' etc. ...

If you don't get along with the phrases you could use the image of the sun once again. Imagine that the soft and warm rays of the sun in your heart are radiating out towards your friend ... you could also imagine that they have a sun in their heart, which is radiating kindness to their whole being ...

You can also use your breath. Imagine that you are breathing in awareness of them, and breathing out your good wishes towards them ...

Do this for some time, and then let them fade from your mind, bring your awareness back to your body and your breath for a few moments ... and bring the practice to a close.

Your experience

Write down your experience of doing this practice.

Who did you choose?

....

What thoughts, if any, did you have as you did the practice?

....

What feelings, if any, did you have as you did the practice?

....

What physical sensations, if any, did you have as you did the
practice?

....

Meditation 10: kindness towards people about whom we feel indifferent

Once you've practised this meditation for some time you can widen your circle of kindness further, to include people you have only a passing acquaintance with. This can be challenging because we don't usually feel very much about people we don't know. Here we have to use our imagination: this person has a life as important to them as your life is to you. Like you, they don't want to suffer, and like you, they want to be healthy and happy.

Do the practice just as you did towards the person you like. That is:

Sit in a comfortable posture, close your eyes and spend some time just being aware of the various sensations in your body ... and so on.

People we find difficult

Other people can be difficult, of course: they don't always do what we want them to – they have minds of their own! It's tempting to try to change them (for their own good of course!), but I expect you've learned from your own experience that that seldom works. It's less frustrating simply to let people be who they are, with all their faults.

When people are critical of us, or treat us badly, the red emotion system is activated in us. This tends to make us defensive or offensive, and if we act on this we can make the situation worse. It's better if we can turn up the green, in which we feel the pain of the other person's behaviour, but are able to step back a bit, and act with a little more wisdom than perhaps we would have if we'd acted from the red. Turning up the green doesn't mean that we allow others to treat us as doormats – we can speak up for ourselves and fight injustices – but we're able to do it more effectively, because we're calmer and emotionally stronger.

So now, let's widen our circle of kindness to include someone we are currently finding difficult – perhaps someone who has treated us badly. To do this meditation effectively we need to have already cultivated a fairly robust sense of self-kindness, otherwise we might be overwhelmed with the hurt this person has caused us, or with anger at their behaviour. In other words, we'll be turning up the red rather than the green.

Meditation 11: kindness to people we find difficult

First, spend some time developing kindness to yourself, then towards someone you care for. That will give you a positive basis on which to develop kindness to the difficult person. You can then bring to mind someone you don't know well, widening your circle of kindness a little further, and finally, the difficult person.

You can do each of the of these stages in much the same way that you did the kindness-to-self and friend meditations. That is:

Sit in a comfortable posture, close your eyes and spend some time just being aware of the various sensations in your body ... and so on.

Spending some time every day cultivating a positive attitude to a difficult person can have a very good effect on yourself, but also in your relationship with that person. Someone who was once an enemy can become a friend. This may seem unbelievable, not to mention undesirable! Well, just practise and see what happens.

Kindness to everyone

Once you've practised in this way with individual people, you can, if you wish, widen your circle of kindness even further to encompass everyone on the planet. Over 7 billion and counting!

Meditation 12: kindness to everyone 🔊

Obviously you're not going to be able to practice this meditation to individuals, as you did in the previous meditations. Instead, bring to mind people in a more general sense, starting with all your friends, relations and colleagues, and then extending to everyone who lives in your town or city, and then your country, continent and the world. You don't have to limit your circle of kindness to people, either; you can include animals, birds, etc., everything that lives.

Do the practice just as you did towards the person you like and the person you are indifferent to. That is:

Sit in a comfortable posture, close your eyes and spend some time just being aware of the various sensations in your body ... and so on.

Mindfulness in action 8: choose to respond rather than react

Near the beginning of this book I said that one of the reasons for practising mindfulness is that it allows us more choice. While we can't always choose what happens to us or how other people behave, we *can* learn to have more choice in how we respond to life's events. Now, as we near the end of the book, and with the benefit of all that practice behind you, I invite you to play with your freedom of choice.

The next time you feel your buttons being pressed, see if you can step back from your reaction, take a few seconds to breathe, and let it go. This isn't easy. Depending on the strength of your reaction, sometimes you'll be able to do it, other times you won't. That's OK, it's a practice. If you found it easy you wouldn't need to practise it.

Those times (there will be many) when you don't manage to let go of your reaction, you need to be careful you don't react to your failure ('You idiot, you've failed again,' etc.). Be careful that your inner critic doesn't have a field day. Instead, just remind yourself that your brain, like everyone else's, is wired like that. It's evolved to react to threats with anger, fear, avoidance, etc., and so it's natural to react.

All the practices you've learned from this book will help you to build up inner resources of awareness, calm, clarity and kindness, that will help you to respond, rather than react. So, in the long term, keep these up as best you can. But right there, at the coalface of your life, you have to try to do it in the most testing of circumstances: someone pushes in front of you in a queue, your printer won't work just when you need it to, a family member is rude to you, your car breaks down, you receive a letter from your energy supplier informing you that they're going to raise their prices (again!), someone at work is dismissive of a job you've done, it's raining (again!) – the list is endless, isn't it? Lots of opportunities to practise! The good news is that the more you practise the easier it becomes. Stimulating the neural substrates of calm, contentment and caring – the green system – strengthens them. This also makes it less likely that your buttons will be pressed.

To get into the swing of responding rather than reacting, you can start choosing to act differently before you find yourself in a difficult situation in which you'd usually react. Once you start making choices in these easier circumstances, you'll feel the freedom of deciding to act differently, and this paves the way (opens up the neural pathways) to respond to things you would normally react to.

Here are a few things you could decide to do – you could choose to:

- take a different route to work

- say hello to someone you usually ignore

- look up at the sky as you're walking along the road

- say something complimentary to someone you find difficult

- be kind to someone when you don't have to be (you don't need a reason)

- buy a gift for someone when it's not Christmas or their birthday

- turn off the TV and read a book instead

- be patient with someone's failings rather than critical

- be patient with your own failings rather than critical.

Choose the life you want.

Summary

In this chapter we've been exploring the green emotion system, especially the connection aspect of that system: the social emotions of kindness, affection, friendliness.

Practice

We've extended the kindness meditation to include other people, starting with those we already feel positively towards, through to everyone on the planet. The final *mindfulness in action* is to choose to respond rather than react.

 To download the templates of journals for this chapter's practices go to www.breathworks-mindfulness.org.uk/the-little-mindfulness-workbook.

9 The rest of your life

As we near the end of this book, it's perhaps time to start considering how you're going to live your life from now on. That is, how will you look after yourself, making sure you have the resources to deal with the various things life will throw at you, so that you're able to maintain a sense of equanimity and tranquil happiness *and* be there for other people when they need you? Another way of putting this is: How will you continue to balance the three emotion systems, making sure that the red and blue systems don't outweigh the green?

Idea: avoiding the exhaustion funnel

You probably know the syndrome: your life is going OK until something happens: you get overloaded at work, a family member falls ill, you fall out with someone, and life suddenly feels too much. You think, 'I can't do everything I usually do this week, something will have to go.' But what? Usually the first thing we drop is something that isn't essential, and that won't entail letting others down very badly: going to the gym, listening to music, seeing a friend, watching a film, reading a book. Something, in other words, that we enjoy, that nourishes us, and that makes us feel glad to be alive.

By the end of the week we're a little more tired, a little more jaded, and perhaps our mood is a bit lower too, because we didn't do one of the things that helps to keep us nourished, although we did continue to do all those things that deplete us and make us feel stressed. So now we feel that something else is going to have to go this week. What? Something else that we enjoy, and that won't let others down very much. As a result, by the end of that week we feel even more depleted, something else has got to go … you can see where this is going, can't you?

The exhaustion funnel

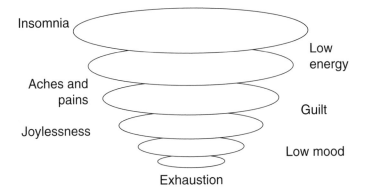

Insomnia

Low energy

Aches and pains

Guilt

Joylessness

Low mood

Exhaustion

The above diagram comes from Professor Marie Åsberg, of the Karolinska Institute, Stockholm. She's an expert on burnout, and this is how she thinks it happens. The top ring of the funnel shows a full life, with work, family, friends, exercise, hobbies and so on. The bottom ring is a life that has been stripped down to those things we have to do merely to stay alive – work, cleaning, food shopping, etc. If we're not careful we'll fall from one ring down to the next, and the next, until we're at the bottom, burned out. Professor Åsberg suggests that those of us who fall down the exhaustion funnel are likely to be the most conscientious workers, whose level of self-confidence is closely dependent on their performance at work, and who are often seen as the best workers, not the lazy ones. Although she refers to 'performance at work' and 'workers', it's easy to see how this syndrome can also apply to other contexts, such as family and friends.

Enquiry 4: sustainers and drainers

Take some time to think about all the things that sustain you – activities that you enjoy and that are life enhancing. Write them down in the left-hand column.

Now consider all the things in your life that tend to drain your energy, that you don't enjoy and that deplete your energy. Write them down in the right-hand column.

Sustainers	Drainers

Now you've done that, you can reflect a little on your life: do the sustainers outweigh the drainers or vice versa?

Of course, figuring that out is not a simple matter of adding up the numbers; you may have listed more drainers than sustainers, for instance, but the drainers may take up much less of your time, or their effect is less than the few sustainers you've listed.

It's more a matter of intuition – do you feel that your life has enough enjoyment and satisfaction? If not, are there ways in which you can reduce the drainers and increase the sustainers? Are there things in your sustainers list that you no longer do, or haven't done for a while? If so, can you bring them back into your life? Or can you turn a drainer into a sustainer? If, for instance, you dislike housework, can you find a way to make it enjoyable and life enhancing?

Continuing to practise

Perhaps you've found the practice of mindfulness to be sustaining. I hope so, and I hope you continue to practise. I've known people to get a lot from learning mindfulness, only to stop practising once they felt better, and guess what happened then? Well, I'm afraid they lost much of what they'd gained. Mindfulness only works to the extent that you practise it.

So the question arises, how will you make sure you do continue to practise? It could be that you get so much from it that you'll never stop, but most of us need a little support, especially at those times when practice feels difficult. One thing you can do is try to find a meditation group near you, preferably one that meets regularly, so that you can join them. You'll need to make sure that you'll be able to continue with the mindful meditations that you've learned in this book, though; some groups insist that you only practise the specific meditations that they do.

Flourishing

The diagram of the exhaustion funnel graphically illustrates what can happen to us if we don't look after ourselves. However, it's a limited picture because it suggests that the best we can hope for is to be OK. But, just as we can 'fall down' the exhaustion funnel, so we can 'rise up' another kind of funnel. I want to end this book with a diagram that illustrates a kind of positive spiral, from being OK, coping with life, to flourishing, creatively responding to whatever life throws at you. Just as the exhaustion funnel narrows as our energy diminishes and our options close down, so the flourishing spiral broadens as we move upwards; the more mindful we are, the more choice we have over our mental and emotional states, the more inner freedom we have. Of course it's not that you'll rise to the top of the spiral and stay there; you'll go up and down that spiral, at times feeling great, while at others weighed down by the burdens that you're having to carry. But on the whole, if you continue to look after yourself and practise, you'll be more likely to be somewhere on that spiral than on the slippery slope of the exhaustion funnel.

The flourishing spiral

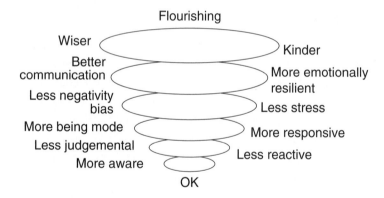

Some things to remember:

- Some suffering is unavoidable, it's an inevitable aspect of being alive.

- Other suffering is optional.

- We can only accept the unavoidable, but we can reduce the avoidable.

- Reacting to unpleasant experiences usually adds to our suffering.

- You don't have to believe everything you think.

- What we resist tends to persist.

- Sometimes to get from A to B, we have to really be at A.

- We have an inbuilt negativity bias, so remember to notice the good things that happen.

Some things to do (be!):

- When possible, do just one thing at a time.

- Pay full attention to what you're doing.

- When the mind wanders from what you're doing, bring it back, gently.

- Don't spend all your time in doing mode spend some time simply being.

- Let in the good.

- Be kind to yourself and to others.

- Repeat the above several billion times.

- Continue to do the practices from this book that have worked for you.

- If you stop doing them (likely!) just start again.

How to use this book as an eight-week course

Ideally, meditate twice a day, and do a *mindfulness in action* many times throughout the day.

Week 1
Meditation: body scan
Mindfulness in action: do one thing mindfully every day

Week 2
Meditation: body scan, mindfulness of breathing and listening to sounds
Mindfulness in action: do something slowly

Week 3
Meditation: mindfulness of breathing – working with thoughts, mindful movement
Mindfulness in action: take a break from activity

Week 4
Meditation: mindfulness of breathing – working with a charged thought, being with an unwanted experience, mindful movement
Mindfulness in action: accept a difficult experience

Week 5
Meditation: choose whichever meditations you wish, with an emphasis on noticing any pleasure you may feel
Mindfulness in action: let in the good

Week 6
Meditation: kindness to self, as well as other meditations of your choice
Mindfulness in action: spend some time in the green circle

Week 7
Meditation: kindness to others meditations, as well as other meditations of your choice
Mindfulness in action: choose to respond rather than react

Week 8 (and onwards!)
Meditation: choose whichever meditations you feel work best for you
Mindfulness in action: be mindful all of the time

Resources

Some books to read:
Here are a few books, relevant to this book, which you might want
to follow up with.

Full Catastrophe Living – Jon Kabat-Zinn (Piatkus).

**Mindfulness for Health: Relieving pain, reducing stress, and
restoring well-being** – Vidyamala Burch and Danny Penman
(Piatkus).

**Mindfulness: A Practical Guide to Finding Peace in a Frantic
World** – Mark Williams and Danny Penman (Piatkus).

Mindfulness for Women – Vidyamala Burch (Piatkus).

The Compassionate Mind – Paul Gilbert (Constable).

The Mindful Path of Self-Compassion – Christopher K. Germer (Guilford Press).

Hardwiring Happiness – Rick Hanson (Rider).

Just One Thing – Developing a Buddha Brain One Simple Practice at a Time – Rick Hanson (New Harbinger Publications).

Love 2.0 – Barbara Fredrickson (Hudson Street Press).

Some websites to visit:
www.breathworks-mindfulness.org.uk
www.bemindful.co.uk
www.freemindfulness.org/download
www.franticworld.com/what-is-mindfulness
www.compassionatemind.co.uk
www.positivityresonance.com/meditations.html
www.rickhanson.net/writings/just-one-thing
www.vidyamala-burch.com

The bestselling general guide to CBT techniques

✓ Overcome problems like stress and anxiety

✓ Re-programme negative thoughts

✓ Focus on positive behaviours to feel good about yourself

A practical introduction to Acceptance and Commitment Therapy

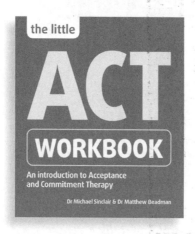

✓ Manage stress, depression and anxiety more effectively

✓ Improve your well-being and resilience

✓ Create an enjoyable, meaningful and fuller life

Get 25% off online! Add LMW01 at checkout.